"For parents, this book give school conferences. It includes much information from the author's seminars for teachers on 'Magic Ways to Talk to Parents.' I recommend that teachers read this perceptive study to learn the most effective conferencing skills."

Jami Owens
Mother and Former Teacher
Legislative Aide, Illinois State Senate
Springfield, Illinois

"A child development book with important information and innovative ideas isn't supposed to be such a fun and easy read. This book has helped me become a better parent and has enhanced my children's lives."

Gary Kutscher
Stay-at-home dad of Nick and Nate
Huntington Beach, California

"This book is fantastic and stands out from the rest of its kind due to the author's sense of humor and personal approach. I found it to be down-to-earth, easy reading. It made me more confident as a mom by helping me fill my daughter's time with easy, beneficial activities."

Stacee Frank
Trophy Club, Texas

GIVE YOUR CHILD AN
Advantage

GIVE YOUR CHILD AN
Advantage

A Witty Exposé on
the Formative Years

SHARON REED

TATE PUBLISHING & *Enterprises*

Published by Tate Publishing & Enterprises, LLC
127 E. Trade Center Terrace | Mustang, Oklahoma 73064 USA
1.888.361.9473 | www.tatepublishing.com

Tate Publishing is committed to excellence in the publishing industry. The company reflects the philosophy established by the founders, based on Psalm 68:11,
"The Lord gave the word and great was the company of those who published it."

Book design copyright © 2008 by Tate Publishing, LLC. All rights reserved.
Cover design by Lindsay B. Behrens
Interior design by Janae J. Glass

Published in the United States of America
ISBN: 978-1-60462-952-1
1. Family & Relationships
2.Education: Preschool & Kindergarten/ Parent Participation
08.04.23

Dedicated to
Kay, Lori, and Art

ACKNOWLEDGMENTS

Thank you to:

Delores Kruger, Lori Huang, Cookie Slavik, and Shelley Angell for their contributions to this book.

The many thousands of parents who have entrusted their beloved children to my care, and to the staff of our centers.

St. Timothy Church, Naperville for their loving care of children.

My own children for giving me grandchildren who are kind, bright, and productive.

God for His awesome blessings.

TABLE OF CONTENTS

15 · Foreword

17 · Introduction

Section I. Home and Family
This is the Easy Part

21 · Preview

23 · How Soon Should I Start to Worry

29 · But He's Messing up the House

33 · But He's Having Another Meltdown

37 · But He's Arguing with Me Again
(a.k.a. I'm Arguing with Him)

41 · They're Ganging up on Me

45 · Will My "Only Child" Be a Lonely Child

Section II. Neighborhood and Beyond
It's Getting Harder

53 · Preview

55 · "Tell Me All About It, Honey"

59 · How Can I Know Whose Fault It Is

65 · How Can I Be Confident About
My Child's Self-Confidence

Section III. Developmental Areas
Now We're Getting Serious

73 · Preview

75 · Is My Child as Smart as I Know He Is

99 · And What If He Is

135 · But What If He Isn't

159 · Is That All There Is

165 · Tell Me About Hansel and the Pop-Up Toaster

Section IV. Child Care and Preschool
Here's the Inside Story

171 · Preview

173 · Give Me the Real Scoop on
Child Care and Preschool

Section V. Kindergarten/School
Early Triumph

211 · Preview

213 · What's a Good Parent to Do

225 · Is Kindergarten Ready for Me

Section VI. The Advantage Factor
What You Can Give Your Child

245 · Preview

247 · The Advantage Factor

Section VII. Conclusion
A Very Happy Ending

263 · Preview

265 · In All This, Where Did I Lose Myself

269 · Will My Child Grow Up and Tell
a Psychiatrist About Me

273 · How Does It All End

FOREWORD

One of the first conversations I had when I arrived in Naperville in the fall of 1987 was with Sharon Reed. Sharon owned and operated the preschool, "Learning Is Fun," that leased space from St. Timothy Lutheran Church. As the new pastor of St. Timothy, I felt that I needed to "have a good feeling" about the director of a preschool that was using our facility and impacting so many families in our community.

At the end of that first conversation I remember feeling that I was in the presence of someone who was wonderfully energetic and passionate about what she did—the care, nurturing, and development of young children. I realized twenty years ago that Sharon exuded a joyful spirit for children, an incredible knowledge and experience with the developmental growth of children, and a deep commitment to helping parents (and other adults) understand how they can enhance that development through informed participation during this vital time in their children's life.

Twenty years later I can honestly state that my earliest assessment of Sharon Reed's passion and knowledge of children, and her deep desire to impart her wisdom to assist parents in giving their children their greatest advantage to a successful life, was right on!

This book *Give Your Child an Advantage* reflects years of her joyful interaction with children; her honest, informed, straightforward conversations with parents; her continuous formal education and research in the field of child development; and her ongoing training and development of teachers. As an observer of literally thousands of children and parents progressing through her preschool during my tenure at St. Timothy, as well as through her chain of daycare facilities—and as a parent who learned so much myself while my own three children were entrusted to Sharon's care during those years—I know firsthand that Sharon has incredible gifts to share in this book.

As you read *Give Your Child an Advantage* you will come to understand and experience what I joyfully witnessed in person for two decades: an optimistic approach to child development which unfolds the gifts of honesty, love, joy, and humor in giving your children a wonderful advantage as they move beyond their early years.

Richard Johnson
Former Senior Pastor
St. Timothy Lutheran Church
Naperville, Illinois

INTRODUCTION

For more than thirty years I have worked with thousands of young children, and I have studied hundreds of teachers and parents working with young children. My educational background is child development, continuous throughout my career. There is much information to share with you, information that can help you *Give Your Child an Advantage*.

First and foremost, you must be convinced that what you do matters. Most children at least muddle through, regardless of their parents' methods. But for your child to be glorious, your methods need to be informed and inspired. You can do this, and this book can guide you. It addresses concerns common to most parents and caregivers of young children; it answers their FAQs and even questions they haven't yet asked.

Your time is valuable. Invest a little of it here, and it will save you hours. Implement some of these methods, and it will make your life incredibly easier and richer.

Some words are used frequently in this book, words such as *fun*. Fun can and should permeate your family life, leading to deep joy. For brevity, *he/him/his* are used for children, and *she/her/hers* are used for adults. And *etc.* is shorthand for a long list of things you don't need detailed.

- The assignment of this book is to give you developmental norms, to give you a context in which to evaluate your child.

- The purpose of this book is to jumpstart your own creativity.

- The promise of this book is that you can do it.

- Your precious child will be glad you did.

Sharon Reed

SECTION I.

HOME AND FAMILY

THIS IS THE EASY PART

PREVIEW

We're laying the groundwork here. It's titled "The Easy Part." You may disagree about how easy it is. Realize that you have more control over things that happen in your home than you will ever have beyond your own threshold.

- In this section, you will learn how most young children progress developmentally, and what should be your main focus for each age.

- If you are to have any energy for giving your child an advantage, you must first take charge of everyday living. Know that you can mold your family with the methods suggested here.

- You will learn an approach to achieving order, accompanied by scary warnings of what your life will be like if you don't.

- Glory be yours…you will read how to minimize meltdowns. Avoiding meltdowns in your child can even result in fewer meltdowns of your own.

- Arguments can be dramatically diminished when you know how to handle them. Read it here.

- Siblings may outnumber you, but they need not overwhelm you. Learn how to view and use rivalry constructively.

- Delve into the same-yet-different world of the "only child."

- This section is playful, but not superficial. It's a caveat that you must get these things in order. It's a warning that if you do not exert the time and effort to be in charge, you will be forever drained of your time and effort trying to fix things that have gone awry.

Amaze yourself—make it happen!

HOW SOON SHOULD I START TO WORRY

Never.

- Worrying may give you wrinkles.

- Worrying may give you gray hair.

- Worrying may give you a troubled child, which could really make you worry.

Instead of worrying, you should:

- Know what is normal child behavior (or misbehavior).

- Evaluate how your child fits those developmental expectations.

- Conceive general goals for your child.

- Make a plan to help him achieve those goals.

- Be creative.

- Have fun with it.

Whether you like it or not, your child will probably grow up to be very much like you. Hopefully you think this is good. Should you have any serious concerns about it, the first place to start the work is with yourself.

Normal behavior for children fits a broad range of predictable developmental patterns. Children generally move through these stages in progressive order, but not necessarily at a pre-assigned age. In other words, not all three-year-olds will exhibit exactly the same functional activities. And to make it more difficult for a parent to understand everything, that developmental achievement does not happen in a straight line upward as you might hope…

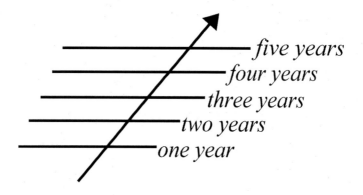

…but in a spiral, gaining ground and then regressing, and gaining even more ground.

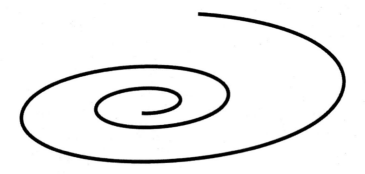

For example, your child may make great progress in potty training, then slide backward, then progress even more. He may start talking, and then stop, and then start again. It need not mean that some elusive negative force is looming to cause regression. It just happens... just as you can golf or bowl like a pro one day, and like an amateur the next. It just happens.

Something your child mastered at three, he may lose several months later—only to regain the skill shortly thereafter. Do not lose heart; you (and your child) will win in the end.

The main developmental concerns for either the parent or the child's caregiver/s are reflected in the following broad categories. Throughout all ages and stages, loving and connecting with your child are understood imperatives.

Early Developmental Functioning

Infant

- Main Focus: health
- Educational Process: communication through all five senses
- Dominant Trait: absorbing everything
- Caregiver Responsibilities: keeping the environment clean and sanitary; monitoring food, meds, and health indicators; using multi-stimulants (hold, talk, rock, sing, etc.)

Toddler

- Main Focus: safety
- Educational Process: exploration
- Dominant Trait: trying everything
- Caregiver Responsibilities: watching constantly; providing a safe, interesting environment; using words

Two-year-old

- Main Focus: independence
- Educational Process: parallel play
- Dominant Trait: oppositional behavior
- Caregiver Responsibilities: setting up an independent play environment; observing and extending parallel play; working toward group play

Three-year-old

- Main Focus: socialization
- Educational Process: group activities (large and small)
- Dominant Trait: making friends
- Caregiver Responsibilities: modeling good social behavior; creating an environment for interactive play; working through social dilemmas

Four-year-old

- Main Focus: expansion
- Educational Process: independent decision-making
- Dominant Trait: activity
- Caregiver Responsibilities: offering individual and group activities; extending social structures; promoting good judgment

Five-year-old

- Main Focus: formal and informal academics
- Educational Process: combining coping and learning skills
- Dominant Trait: inquiring
- Caregiver Responsibilities: creating stimulating learning structures; combining social and intellectual activities; evaluating academic progress

It is not the purpose of this book to detail every age-appropriate activity and characteristic of children. Such books, perhaps necessary but perhaps tedious, are available everywhere. Micromanaging your child can be overwhelming and likely unsuccessful. Rather, this list gives you broad developmental areas to help you decide priorities. Besides, you have more important things than studying intensely about what to do with your child—you have to do it, ready or not.

BUT HE'S MESSING UP THE HOUSE

Unless you want to spend the rest of your life as the designated cleaning lady, or unless you want to live in eternal chaos, you need to get a handle on this now. You can work within the framework of your child's natural behavior and still help him form good habits. It's easiest if the now is while he's still very young.

Very young children dump everything, and then determine not to play with it. But for them, dumping is the play. So make it simple for your child and for yourself. Gather a variety of containers. Buy some inexpensive plastic things, eat ice cream and save the tubs, munch Pringles and use the empty tubes. And give your child fun items to put in the containers. Young children love variety; they love new things. (Paradoxically, they can be put off by a new place at the table, a different bathroom, furniture rearranged, new food. This disorientation is, for most children, only a stage.) Cut a round hole in the plastic lid of a Pringles tube and let your child drop straws inside. Caution: do not be inspired to cover the tube with fancy contact paper, ribbon, or leftover scrapbooking materials. The purpose here is to make it quick and easy, not to be so involved with creating toys that you have little time to play with your child.

Use your child's natural developmental yearning for dumping to inspire order—the only order he can comprehend. Put toys in things. Buy a small plastic wagon or use a large box as the collector, moving it among his toys. Have your child dump things from one container to another, ending up with toys housed in the largest container. Voila! Order comes to your house. Cover the box (whatever) with a blanket, or close the lid on the toy box (if you can). Now, this is tidy for a very young child.

As your child matures, or horrors, if you have already missed the early training years, you can help him form more sophisticated tidying or organizational habits. Lay the groundwork by examining your child's natural functioning. Some children prefer all toys to be visibly available, the Inventory System. If this describes your child, display his toys on shelves—anything from expensive commercial low bookcases to makeshift shelving and hooks within your child's reach. Oh yes, a place for everything and everything in its place.

Of course, only a few children fall into this category. Most children prefer the Rummage System, whereby all toys are dumped in together and dumped out together. With this system, the time of actual play seems to be in inverse proportion to the number of toys. Therefore you can best teach tidying habits by limiting the number of toys in a container. Again inexpensive plastic crates, or even cardboard boxes, can help. Put only a few toys in a container, and make available only a few containers at a time for your child. Hide the others; really hide them. And do not give in. This may be your life's best chance to mold a tidy child, one who can actually find stuff he will need when he's president of some huge company. Switch the boxes periodically to offer your child an exciting "new" world of toys. Whether your child has several dozen toys, or several rooms full of toys, he can be overwhelmed with over-choice. Only when your child has exhibited some mastery of toy usage, focus, and order should you increase the numbers available at one time.

Naturally your involvement in cleaning up or keeping order can make the task ever so much more fun—for your child, not necessarily for you. Whatever methods you conceive, see what works. You may sit near the collector box and have your child bring a toy to you to drop in the box. You may set a timer, trying to beat the clock with cleanup. You make take turns with your child placing a toy in the box. You may sing a cleanup song (make up some song, he'll be intrigued). Encourage him. Bribe him, if necessary; offer rewards of reading him a book, or something. This is sanctioned here because you are rewarding positive, not negative, behavior. Use your own methods, but stand firm. If your child absolutely will not respond to any psychology you use, let him know you will take the toys away. If he still does not respond, put the toys away. Away, as in up high enough your child cannot reach them, for a short time. And remind yourself that you are forming tidying habits—not neurotic, of course, but manageably tidy. Remember, this is after the toddler stage, as a child moves into the twos or threes.

By four years of age, if your child still hasn't discovered the joy of order, you may need to take more desperate measures.

> *One mother, who had little success teaching her four-year-old to be tidy, bought a big plastic laundry basket. Whenever her son dropped something on the floor, she put it in the basket. Shoes, a bat, toys, his favorite book, a prized flashlight, his swimming trunks, etc. (and I do mean etc., etc., etc. Every parent knows about etc. with dropped possessions). You realize how hard it is when you travel and must live out of a suitcase. Think how frustrating it is for a five-year-old to live out of a laundry basket. Eventually this mother had to increase her set to two laundry baskets, but she never had to expand to three. Children do, after all, have some standards, or at least a strong need to find swim trunks to wear to swim lessons.*

While your child is young, tame the beast! Whoa now…the beast does not mean your child; it means clutter, disorganization, and chaos.

All this must be done with a smile on your face, a song on your lips, and hope in your heart.

Sure.

BUT HE'S HAVING
ANOTHER MELTDOWN

Children do, of course. They have meltdowns when they are frustrated, tired, seeking attention, or not getting their way.

But they do it most often if they discover that it works. What works is when someone, some adult in charge, gets worried and doesn't know how to handle it.

That doesn't mean you, because you will know how to handle anger appropriately when, or if, your child has a meltdown.

First you must stay calm. We're talking here about teaching your child to get control of himself at home. You need to know the nature of the melt-down to decide your appropriate response. Your short-term goal is to stop this demonstration at this moment; your long-term goal is to teach your child better ways to be effective. But for now, he's young, and you must stay calm.

If your child has learned that a meltdown results in getting what he wants from you, even some of the time, it will be worth another try. Do not reward the meltdown by buying the toy or giving the candy, etc. The more un-learning that must be done, meaning the more frequently you have rewarded meltdowns in the past, the more work you have to do here. Be brave, and say no. Say it with the confidence that he will survive. Don't shout, don't get angry, don't lose it yourself; just say no. In extreme cases, you may need to keep your child safe from himself. Do what you need to do, and say no.

This is not a complicated system for you to master. If your child is having a meltdown:

Do Not Say This	Instead Say This
How many times have I told you...	No
But it's too close to dinner and I don't have enough cookies for dessert and you'll get chocolate on your clothes and your sister will want one also...	No
If you stop crying, I'll buy you the toy you want...	No
It looks like you're having a meltdown...	No
You're making me unhappy, mad, sad, frustrated, etc...	No

Do not choose alternatives in column A for these reasons:

i. Young children are very literal. Asking, "How many times have I told you..." sends your child's thinking on a tangent (two times, four times, do we count yesterday or just today?) This is not the route you want him to take for clear reasoning. And anyway, it doesn't matter how many times. Two does not make it right; three does not make it wrong.

2. Remember high school English class run-on sentences? Run-on dialogue gets points off too. The official off-limits term is circumlocution. Your child can be so overwhelmed with words, words, words, that he loses any lesson. Prolonged debate should be left for a calmer moment.

3. This meltdown may end with your capitulation, but it will rise again another day...and another...and another...if it is rewarded.

4. Understanding the underlying contributing factor for your child's meltdown is a loving, empathetic parental response. Keep it to yourself at this time. Saying it to your child gives him license to continue and dilutes his incentive to reason. If the underlying cause is real, try to avoid it for your child in the near future. Later when your child is calm, and if he is mature enough to understand, you can have conversations about appropriate ways to express himself and to deal with anger.

5. An official label makes his meltdown official. Do not validate a meltdown within earshot of your child.

6. This is not about you. There are appropriate times to discuss with your child how his

actions affect other people. The passion of his meltdown is not one of those times.

Should you believe that your child is truly out of control, unable to stop crying, use some method of gaining self-control with him. Develop an effective deep-breathing system, or some means of focusing his drama or trauma elsewhere, until the trauma runs its course. Just do not be lured into rewarding this behavior. Whenever you suspect that your attention is prolonging the meltdown, stop responding and ignore your child. It's hard, but it's the right thing to do.

When the meltdown is over, hug, smile, and be silly together. Make the good times so far outweigh the difficult that your child will want to stay in that mode.

Remember in this chapter we are talking about getting control of the situation at home. Meltdowns may still happen, but with diminishing frequency. If you have established good habits at home, your child will be less apt to test you before the world—such as at the grocery store or at the mall. If meltdowns before the world are a recurring problem, take your child home and go back to paragraph five in this chapter, which begins, "First you must stay calm."

BUT HE'S ARGUING WITH ME AGAIN (A.K.A. I'M ARGUING WITH HIM)

By definition, an argument must have more than one person. Your child can only argue with you when you argue with him.

Don't.

When you argue with your child, no one wins; everyone loses.

Begin by taking words seriously. No means no; yes means yes. I'll decide later does not mean I'll decide now. Maybe or not now do not mean yes, but they can be confusing to a child. Aren't you confused at this point? Not every request from your child requires an immediate high-level summit conference.

> *A conscientious parent, wanting to be sure her child developed a strong sense of independence, read child psychology books on giving choices. One recommendation was that if you had something you really wanted your child to choose, you listed that option last, and the child would be most likely to make that his choice. Mother wanted her son to eat soup for lunch, so she asked the question, "Sam, do you want hot dogs or soup for lunch?" Sam said, "No."*

Giving your child choices can be an admirable thing. Run amuck, this becomes frustrating over-choice. When you do give choices, make them limited and simple. Listen to his preferences, but do not let him get mired in indecision. Someone in the family has to be the final decision maker; better it be you than your child. He is not old enough to manage the family.

Of course it's important that you make decisions fairly. Do not, however, take this obligation too far. Often parents, in an effort to assuage their conscience for saying no, sadly tell their child that life is not always fair. The reality is that your child would not want life to be fair. If life were fair, your child would have to give up a whole lot.

> *A very loving mother called me at home one evening to ask for our school's recipe for M&M cookies. I wondered why, and I asked her. She sorrowfully told me that when we served M&M cookies for snack that day, the little girl sitting next to her child had a cookie with more M&Ms than her own daughter's cookie. Her daughter was so sad that Mother was going to bake a batch with lots of M&Ms so her child would no longer be sad.*

A loving mother indeed. But wait ... do not dampen the joy of life for your child. Rejoice, even if his cookie has fewer M&Ms than his sister's. Instill perspective.

Consistency is important, but we've been told about the flaws inherent in a "foolish consistency." Children are comfortable with certain predictability. Usually you need to stand your ground, but some things are not worth bickering about. You need to decide which is which, on the spot, dozens of times a day. Whew! Rules and practices can be temporarily set aside, but should not be done frivolously and without your child understanding the special reason for the dispensation (i.e. "You may stick your tongue out at Grandma now because you are singing this silly song together, but of course we won't do that at other times." Values have not been abandoned here simply because consistency has been trumped.) Fight every impulse within yourself to set aside your rules or your best judgment simply because your child has worn you down. Your child probably was born with the instinct of erosion—erosion of your will. Once it starts, it's progressively easier to wear away. Determine not to become the personification of the Grand Canyon.

The ability to resolve conflict is a valuable life skill. There are numerous methods for teaching conflict resolution skills to parents and to children. You would do yourself and your child a great favor by studying one or more of these systems. Even the most perceptive parent can learn a great deal. Some possible options are: "Raising a Thinking Child," "Systematic Training for Effective Parenting," "I Can Problem Solve," "1-2-3 Magic." Most methods target a specific age group, and some target specific behavior patterns. In some communities, grade schools teach and use a particular conflict resolution method. You may want to call your child's future school to inquire about this.

Whatever you do, do it now.

THEY'RE GANGING UP ON ME

No parent of more than one child needs a definition of sibling rivalry. You just need help.

When asked what they do to get their way from a brother or sister, siblings answer these things: hit, sit on, chase, kick, boss, cry, threaten, bite, pull hair, complain to parent, scream, grab something away, scratch, bribe. Does this sound like a youth mafia?

That's the bad news. The good news is that, coming from a normal home, children rarely carry true resentment toward siblings into their adulthood. Usually these practices are reduced to "horsing around" in the memory of a child grown up. In the meantime, you, the parent, have to survive, sanity intact, to lead your children to greater glory—or at least to the age of majority, relatively unscathed.

The other good news is that a certain degree of sibling rivalry is not only normal, but builds in a safe buffer for conflict in personal relationships and competition in the world as your children grow up.

Birth order can play a big role in the nature of sibling rivalry. The first child, being one-and-only for a time, can be understandably threatened by the arrival of a new baby. Imagine if your spouse brought home a rival for your position. No amount of advance press would really convince you that "you're going to love it."

The second and all subsequent children never know this exact position, but any child can feel disadvantaged by siblings. Sometimes rightfully so.

General characteristics of birth order have been charted, and they are interesting. Firstborn children are often more reserved and introspective, secondborn children are frequently described as more independent and expressive, the middle child can feel squeezed by both ends, youngest children can be outgoing and daring. Of course these are only generalities; each of your children has his own personality. And if you are parents of an "only child," you can still read this chapter to be an expert for your friends' family affairs—or should you have miscalculated your future prolificacy.

It is healthy and fun for you to have special time with each child alone. This can be as simple as a private story time before bed, or as elaborate as a day together at the zoo. Family times with joyful activities, all together or with various special pairings, can bond siblings to a lifelong unit far stronger than self-interest.

Coping with sibling rivalry calls on your greatest patience and wisdom. While acknowledging individual differences in your children, you will not want to take the easy way out by always allowing the strongest-willed child to rule by force, the loudest to rule by volume, the smartest to rule by cunning, or the youngest to rule by default.

But it's okay if you sometimes just don't have the energy to figure out which is which. You are not obligated to conduct a full-scale trial to settle every incident. Remember that conflict resolution training can turn a squabbling family into a manageable mix. And children may surprise you and settle their own differences, to their mutual satisfaction.

As long as you truly love each child, and try to be reasonably fair most of the time, it will work out in the end. Of course, the end doesn't happen until the kids all grow up and move out.

WILL MY "ONLY CHILD"
BE A LONELY CHILD

Sometimes, yes. But everyone is lonely sometimes, and that's not always negative. Alone time can nurture the greatest thoughts, creativity, and inspiration... even for a child.

Like many things in life, being an only child has good news/bad news.

The obvious good points of having no siblings include:

- No competition for parents' attention
- No one taking your stuff
- Having your own bedroom, etc.
- Spending the entire family discretionary income and inheritance
- Never having to say, "I'm sorry"
- Being the center of the world, or at least the eternal star of the family

The bad points include:

- Hmmmmm, it may be hard to find fault with this above system ... hmmmmm

Seriously, being one of a family group can bring a blessed reassurance. When the children are rowdy,

Mom or Dad can shout, "You kids quiet down." The siblings then can giggle and commiserate; the blame is not personal. On the other hand, when an only child is reprimanded, it is unavoidably personal—it's you, kid…you and you alone, no matter how kindly the parent may say it. No in-house group therapy available here. Parents need to find a balance between making the only child feel responsible without feeling guilty. Either extreme can be harmful.

Just as sibling support can empower, sibling scathing can deflate. An only child may not have these opposites, lovingly dispensed, to desensitize him. If your only child is too tender for the world, use humor and reassurance as you inure him.

Only children are more often the family decision maker. "Where do you want to go to eat?" "What movie do you want to see?" "What do you want for snack?" "What game do you want to play?" Try getting a consensus from several children within the same family…ha! In a threesome with Mom, Dad, and only child, the only child may actually wield the most sway. Thus, he may need extra practice at being the minority vote.

Extended family groupings as in days of yore are a rare scene today. Obviously play dates are even more important for the only child, as are preschool and religious classes and team sports and neighborhood play. Be aware that play dates in your own home still make your only child king of the hill: the toys are his, the house rules are his, the turf is his.

He needs experience at being the guest in someone else's realm as well.

Parents of an only child may fear spoiling their child. Spoiling is a word used as an oversimplification of a complex concept. Any child, the only child or one of many, can be jaded by too many possessions. Any child can be disoriented by lack of appropriate discipline, or lack of a social conscience. Any child can be confused and disappointed in a world that does not fulfill his expectations of deference toward him. These pitfalls are just more difficult for parents of the only child to avoid. There are some built-in safeguards with larger families; it's hard to be too smug amid siblings.

The syndrome of the too-precious child is not exclusive to the only child. Decades ago, when most families were large, parents surely loved their children as much as we do today. They simply could not invest all their thought and limited treasure as exclusively as we can today. Yes, your child is the most precious thing in the world...and so is every other child (paradox). Your child is so precious that he must enjoy all the truths of the universe, including his rightful role. Because we have so many blessings, it's easy to heap them all on our children, which can be daunting if there is only one recipient.

As your only child matures, you may want to give some thought to enabling him to form a few deep friendships. Not all brothers and sisters form loving bonds to last a lifetime, but the only child doesn't even have that possibility with siblings. Thus he especially can benefit from a living history with others his age, from shared memories of his growing up. As you age and your only child grows into the role of nurturer, he will enjoy someone with whom to reminisce.

Do not fear; your only child can be generous and considerate and appreciative. If you have proper goals and good sense, if you help your child accurately define his rightful role, your only child will be well adjusted.

The world readily acknowledges that a dozen children take all the parents' time. A seldom mentioned diminution for you is that the world doesn't always realize that one child also takes all the parents' time—and he does. If you, as an only child parent, do not feel duly respected, show any doubters this paragraph.

Summary

For your child, it all begins in the home. Whether he spends his days with you, or with other caregivers, *you* are the greatest influence on your child's development.

Laugh, sing, dance, talk, get silly, try new things. If you're not having fun, you're not doing it right.

In order for your child to be successful in life, certain fundamentals must be reasonably mastered.

You must stay calm and confident. Anything less will adversely affect. You can do this; no one loves your child more than you do. Knowing what to expect and how to handle situations can be learned. There is wonderful information available to help you in all areas of child development. Find some method that fits your parenting style.

A minimum sense of order is necessary to function effectively. Help your child learn some degree of tidiness and order so that you all can get on with joyous family living.

Meltdowns mean out of control. Teach your child better ways to make things happen in his life.

Do not run your household through arguments. Use good conflict resolution methods, and your child will learn to negotiate to his advantage. Remember that no one really wins an argument; when families argue constantly, everyone loses.

Ignore harmless sibling rivalry; control harmful sibling rivalry. The trick is knowing the difference. Working within the framework of your children's individual personalities, teach good conflict resolution methods. Teach both by instruction and role modeling.

An only child needs special direction in a few areas.

If any of these categories is deeply flawed—change it, fix it.

When this framework of effective functioning has been established in the home, you have begun to *Give Your Child an Advantage.*

SECTION II.

NEIGHBORHOOD & BEYOND

IT'S GETTING HARDER

PREVIEW

Now that your child is ready to go out into the world, you are ready for the next body of information. "It's Getting Harder" because there are so many more components, and fewer of them are under your control.

- In this section you will learn ways to teach your child the process of clear thinking and problem solving, to his great advantage.

- The wisdom of separating facts from emotions, and a method of dealing with each, is detailed.

- Read how to handle lies versus truth, with a system to use both productively.

- Learn the shortcomings of assigning blame.

- Gain an understanding of the full reality of sharing.

- Jumpstart your own creativity with the various plans for inspiring productive behavior and eliminating destructive behavior in your child.

- Discover how to imbue your child with true self-confidence.

"TELL ME ALL ABOUT IT, HONEY"

As your child ventures into the world, you can help.

In everyday living, you interpret the world for your young child. It works ever so much better if you do it right.

Thoughts and feelings are both important as you try to figure out life. The ability to separate them allows you, and by extension your child, to view things accurately.

In recent decades, much value has been placed on "expressing your feelings" or "getting it all out." A question frequently asked of children is, "How do you feel about that?"

Feelings are important. But feelings not based in fact can take on a life of their own, sometimes leading down a path to nowhere. If your child is exhibiting emotion—hurt, anger, crying, frustration, rage—your first reaction must be to love and comfort. As you soothe and validate his feelings, do not merge those feelings with the facts of the event.

As soon as your child is calm, help him discern the difference between what really happened and how he feels about what really happened. You can start with a simple statement, "Let's talk about what really happened."

Teach your child the *Step Thinking Process*:

Step Thinking Process	
Ask your child…	
What happened first	1. He answers
Then what happened	2. He answers
What happened next	3. He answers

Even if your child is too young to read, he can benefit from your writing down these steps. The power of paper, you know. Write a big 1 and enter his first "this happened" thought. As he answers "then what happened," continue writing his steps.

If your child is too distracted to wait for the writing, try having him hold up fingers: one finger as you discuss the first thing that happened, etc. Model if necessary; it doesn't matter if he holds up the wrong number of fingers.

You may need to make corrections to this story. That's okay. In review, you may ask, "Is that what really happened?" You can judge if you hear a ring of truth—or not.

An important component of the *Step Thinking Process* is that you use only action words: he did, I said, they ran away. Avoid the emotional, feeling words: blame, anger, regret, sorrow, pity; these can interfere with clear thinking. Your purpose here is to establish the truth, just the facts. If your child is reluctant to discuss anything when you first try this process, it may be because emotion and shame have been felt previously in this discussion situation. If this be the case, you may need to put things into your own words and ask him if that is right. It may take numerous tries. When your child feels safe in this discussion, it will happen. Hang in there. This is a process, not a quick fix.

You need not be unduly disturbed if your young child tells untrue facts, things that never happened. Your daily world can be routine and uneventful; a child's pretend world of fancy may be even more enticing to you than your own—but then, who would do the laundry?

Do not fear that your preschool-aged child is telling lies. Help him acknowledge the difference. When he says something you suspect or know not to be true, help him by asking, "Did that really happen, or are we pretending that it happened?" Not, "Are we *just* pretending that it happened?" You need not overvalue pretending, but label it as such and accept it without fear.

If your child continues to merge truth and fiction without distinction, try making your two columns and writing down:

This Really Happened	This is Pretend
His detail	His detail
Etc.	

After discussion, you may want to move a tale from one column to the other.

Again, the power of paper: a record ever so much

more respected and permanent than spoken words alone.

When you have established the facts as you and your child believe them to be, only then should you discuss the appropriate feelings, the right-and-wrong moral stand as you see it.

It's a normal human yearning to be right and to be loved. Therefore if your child denies a wrongdoing, you can understand his motive. When he says, "I didn't bite my friend Jamie," and Jamie actually has your child's teeth marks on her arm, the lie must be addressed. If you value truth more than you value a cover-up, your child will know.

You have the right and the responsibility to convey your moral beliefs to your child. Actually, this will happen whether you intend to do it or not.

HOW CAN I KNOW
WHOSE FAULT IT IS

If you are a normal parent, you know it's not your child's fault. Period. Unless, of course, it's a problem between your own children, in which case it gets harder to point the Finger of Fault.

Yes, yes...he learned it from the boy next door...he's tired...the other boy hit him first...he didn't get his turn...his teacher doesn't understand him...*zzzzz* (wake me when it's over).

Searching for blame, indeed even assigning blame (rightly or wrongly), will do little good for your child. It may do wonders for your guilt complex, but it really won't help your child.

What will work is starting with the *Step Thinking Process* and then discussing possibilities and consequences. Once you have established the facts, as your child has related them, you can brainstorm: Why do you think he did that? What did you want to happen? What could you have done differently? What do you think might have happened then? What do you think you might try if something like this happens again?

You see, there will always be children who kick. There will always be children who taunt. There may frequently be a birthday party to which your child is not invited. When the world does not conform to his wishes, when he doesn't win the prize, when someone rejects him, the appropriate response is, "Oh, well…" Life has lots of "oh, well…" opportunities. "Oh, well…" should not be used as giving up on life, but in realizing when there are more important issues than these.

You cannot referee the world. You can teach your child good negotiating skills. If he's lucky, you will.

Even in your own home and within your own family, you cannot always be the God of Fairness and Justice. It's okay if sometimes you are too tired or too busy to stop and figure it all out. Remember this advice: It works best if you teach by teaching, not by correcting. That means it's hard to bring calm discussion to screaming siblings. Teach discussion and negotiating skills when emotions are not explosive, when your child is not hoping a critical verdict will be handed down—in his favor. It must be a teachable moment.

Some parental action must be taken at times, using the situation to reinforce your morals and expectations. It's always best if this can be phrased in positive terms (i.e. "It would be good if you would share.") Negative judgments can bring a defensive reaction in your child; that's how it usually works in adults, and they should know better.

Use words accurately. "Sharing," for example, needs to include a willingness on the part of the one who gives over. So when you forcibly take something from one child to give to another, that is not sharing. It's assuredly all right for you to do this, just don't tell your child it's sharing. You rightfully say, "It's good to share," as you make this happen, and hope in time your child will choose to do this on his own. Sharing is not a concept very young children understand. Some children have little reluctance to give over a toy to a playmate and move on to something else. This could be because they understand the sharing concept; likely it's because they don't care so much, because they are compliant, or because they just don't want a confrontation. Other children struggle, and indeed are even more lured to a toy pre-possessed by another child. If you ask, "Who had it first?" you may only confuse both children attracted to the same toy. In their minds, first could mean yesterday, or initially when it was purchased, or earlier this morning. What does that mean, first? You may rightfully say, "Johnny was playing with this. We'll give it to you in one minute," or something else appropriate for your child's understanding. Taking turns can be an easier concept for children to accept.

Certain days, wise old Solomon may not live at your house. In that case, you need Plan BB.

If all else fails and you near desperation, have at the ready a Bonkers Bag (Plan BB). When the spaghetti boils over on the stove, the telephone rings, your mother-in-law shows up unexpectedly at your front door, and your five-year-old is screaming because your three-year-old just flushed the goldfish down the toilet, reach for the Bonkers Bag. Just before you go bonkers. In this bag you will in advance have put something that will delight and occupy your children. It need not be expensive or elaborate, but it must be something he can do without your supervision or detailed instruction, and it must be something that will fascinate him for more than thirty seconds. Think ahead—what might work? A lightweight disposable plastic plate and cup; he bounces the cup high in the air with the plate as a paddle. Show him once, he's got it. Pinch clothespins (remember clothespins?) can be attached to a can. A box can be decorated with colored post-it notes. Straws can be connected with pipe cleaners. Paint-with-water pages torn from a book can be used with a brush and small amount of water. Little cars can run on tracks of yarn spread throughout the house. Paint swatch samples from a hardware store can be matched with the cars, or with each other. A tweezers used to pick up paperclips. Miniature marshmallows to be structured together with toothpicks. Magnets. Anything your creative mind can imagine. It doesn't have to be some fantastic new toy; it just needs to be at the ready. P.S. Your child is not allowed to ask for the Bonkers Bag. And never let him know how it is "earned."

Plan BB can lead your child from wreaking havoc and wrecking the house to productive activity. This pattern can be carried forward to the larger world, making your child admired and making you proud.

Television and computers can be easy, ready answers to your child's discontent, and they can be great entertainment and learning tools for him. They also can be the good news-bad news answers; you understand why. However much these electronic wonders may interest your child, they must not be the only activities that amuse him. Don't let your child be so absorbed into a virtual world that he misses the real world.

A child can think of only one thing at a time; it's true. Attention may flit from one thing to another, but if he's actively involved in something productive, it's less likely he will be destructive.

Sometimes you and your child are trapped. You go to a restaurant, where apparently their last waiter walked off the job ten minutes before you were ready to order. (You've been to that restaurant, haven't you?) So you sing songs with your child, you talk to him, you recite nursery rhymes together...till your repertoire and your patience are both exhausted. You may even have brought some of his favorite toys to amuse him, which during this extensive wait no longer amuse him. Let him build a tower with butter and cream containers. Let him join straws together by pinching one end. Let him put spoons in empty cups. If you get desperate, let him shake a little salt and pepper together on a dish. Let him smash saltines in their little plastic bag by rolling a glass over it. Fold napkins in different ways. Count silverware; match spoon for spoon. Hide a piece of silverware under a napkin and try to guess which it is (spoon, fork, knife). Guess the color of a hidden sweetener packet, or make patterns of pink, blue, brown, and white packets. This is productive; screaming and crashing into other would-be diners is not. If that makes you feel too guilty, leave a slightly more generous tip.

You are not expected to provide 24/7 entertainment for your child. Self-comfort is a worthy attribute for your child to develop. But in a pinch, be there.

At least whatever happens, it won't be *your* fault.

HOW CAN I BE CONFIDENT ABOUT MY CHILD'S SELF-CONFIDENCE

Everyone must work within the framework of his own personality, even children. Some individuals are naturally more reserved, and others naturally outgoing, and that's fine. It's not the goal to change your child's basic personality.

It is important to be sure your child's level of participation in the world is his true choice, that he is not holding back out of fear or lack of confidence…or surging forward out of compulsion beyond his control.

A generation of parents has worked hard to instill self-confidence in their children by avoiding criticism and lavishing praise. While this was carried out with good motives, the method too often went awry. We developed what is known as "praise junkies." That is, too many children were dependent on someone else, usually their parents or teachers, which later they transferred to their peers, to validate them with approving words or nods.

When you love and praise your child, you develop his confidence in you. Only when your child does something himself can he develop confidence in himself. That's why we call it "self-confidence."

Use words that help him validate his own person.

"I love you" is important, but it serves a purpose different from, "You made a friend." "I'm proud of you" makes him love you; "You must be proud of what you did" helps him love himself. It's great to say, "I like your picture," but don't forget sometimes to say, "You worked hard on this picture," or "I can see you like yellow," or "You've learned to make circles!" or even "How do *you* like your picture?"

If you think your child would benefit from being more outgoing, less afraid of taking a risk, more sure of himself—make it happen. This does not involve your pushing a reticent child. It does require your plotting and planning.

Wherever your child is functioning comfortably, think of a way to lead him to the next step.

If he is shy with clerks at the supermarket, give him a dollar (if a dollar can buy anything these days) to pay for a candy bar he has selected himself.

Invite another child and his mother to your house for coffee some morning. Your child will make a friend on his own home ground. This is a real door opener for your child, eventually extending to other places and even to other children he meets.

Arrange to take your child and another child to a movie together, or to a park together. Depending on the children's ages, the other child's parent may need to go along. This is slightly different from a play date, since your child is the host—a little one-upmanship, which translates into a little more confidence.

Call or visit (alone) your local fire department and ask if you can take your child there to see the fire trucks and meet a firefighter. Be sure arrangements are finalized in advance (barring an unexpected fire run). Be certain the person with whom you plan understands that your child is shy, and be sure that the firefighter you will meet will want to talk with your child. And try not to have the word "shy" used in your child's hearing.

You can do this same procedure with police officers, the post office, the local convenience store, an ice cream shop, a pizza parlor, whatever is of interest to your child. Watch him become "the young man about town." Of course, you need to make arrangements in advance, go at a time convenient for the merchant or community service person, and be sure the person you are scheduled to meet will be friendly. And don't forget to say so your child *can* hear, "Thanks. We had fun."

If your child hides behind your back, you may hold him for security. If your child will not speak, free him by assuring, "It's okay to…tell the firefighter your name…tell the lady you're three years old…" wherever the conversation leads, but you need not force him. Your calm and confidence can encourage him. Even if your child does not participate to the level you would like, he has internalized that the world will be a friendly place when he's ready. Be assured that someday he *will* talk— perhaps nonstop.

Laughter is always a heart warmer. You can tell your child a story or two about when you were his age. This falls into the category of truths that never happened, a.k.a. untrue facts (see Chapter 7). Only this time you don't have to tell him it's pretend. You're allowed to use constructive denial here, for the greater benefit of your child.

> *Tell him about the time you were afraid to step on the lawn of the man who lived on the corner. Other children said he would yell at anyone who came near his yard. One day, as you passed by, the man came out, with a big dog! You were so scared, too scared even to run. But the man smiled and waved, and asked if you knew his dog Sandy. He didn't yell. You couldn't believe it. When you got home from school, you told your mother and she said, "Oh, that's old Mr. Jones. He's so nice." Then you told your mother how afraid you had been. She said, "Oh, how silly!" And you both laughed.*

If someone as grand as his parent could overcome fear, your child will believe he can too. And he can...with your patience and help. Your confidence is contagious. Unfortunately so is your lack of confidence. If your child detects fear in your heart, he will have terror in his own. If your child detects pity on your face, he will have sorrow on his own. If you are not sure of things, however can your child have confidence? And it's hard to kid a kid. Be brave for your child; it will do wonders for you too.

Summary

Just when you have everything nearly perfect in your home and family, it's time for your child to go out into the world. Hopefully your insight and influence have produced a glorious child.

As your child leaves your hand, remember:

You interpret the world for your child. Make it good. Love and comfort him, but also teach him to think clearly. Using the Step Thinking Process, develop in him the ability to reason well. Discuss moral rights and wrongs in a positive way, teaching but not assigning guilt at too young an age. If your child tells things that never happened, allow it. Just be sure he differentiates between true facts and pretend.

Pointing the Finger of Fault is hardly productive; often it matters less whose fault it is and more how your child can best handle a situation. Try to be fair without being paranoid, and entertaining without being exhausted. If you are exhausted, go to Plan BB.

Using the right words can help your child develop confidence not just in you, but in himself. Even if your child is shy, you can help him discover the world as a friendly, affirming place. Phone a friend.

To develop a right-reasoning and confident child, your insight and confidence are necessary. If you think you can, or you think you can't—either way, you've got it.

SECTION III.

DEVELOPMENTAL AREAS

NOW WE'RE GETTING SERIOUS

PREVIEW

"Now We're Getting Serious" because your child's developmental progress is important.

Want to know how your child "measures up"?

To get insight into your child's abilities, read about the various intelligences.

You can assess your child's kindergarten readiness with the evaluation games in the areas of:

- Auditory Functioning
- Visual Functioning
- Small Motor Skills
- Large Motor Skills
- Language Skills

With this information, you will be able to select the right activities to help your child soar. Whether you settle on "What If My Child Is as Smart as I Think He Is," or "What If He Isn't," or possibly some of each, you can use the myriad suggestions to have fun with your child as he progresses.

Learn about the three personality types of children, as well as the three components that determine your child's developmental evolution.

And see what your attitude can do!

IS MY CHILD AS SMART
AS I KNOW HE IS

There are all kinds of smarts, and all have value. Intelligence can be social, having real savvy about people and situations. Intelligence can be creative, with inspired receptors for music and art in all forms. Intelligence can be good sense, street smarts, logic. Intelligence can be communicative, with keen linguistic ability and emotional connections. Intelligence can be scientific and mathematical. Intelligence can be kinetic, with outstanding physical skill and/or understanding of motion. Intelligence can be spiritual, with a unique connection to goodness and understanding. Intelligence can be practical, making things work.

It's not unusual for a child who has high intelligence in one area to have lower performance abilities in another area. It would be risky for you to assume that your child's high or low ability at a preschool level will necessarily follow him forever. As children develop, some characteristics have more permanence than others, and all characteristics can evolve at their own pace. Every kind of intelligence is a blessing. But the kind parents most often assess for children is scholastic and time sensitive:

How early did he start talking?

How young did he start walking?

When is he going to be potty trained?

Can he read yet?

How high can he count?

Can he write his name? In D'Nealian?

In Cursive?

Is he ready for kindergarten?

Parents: Before reading the next section, you should write on the chalkboard one hundred times:

1. Kindergarten readiness is not the same thing as intelligence.

2. Kindergarten readiness is not the same thing as intelligence.

3. Kindergarten readiness is not the same thing as intelligence.

The following norms are general guidelines for school readiness; do not isolate specific functions to make any judgment about your child's overall ability. Bear in mind that this focus is extremely limiting in evaluating your child's intelligence or predicting adult success. It does, however, tell some things we want to know. Especially as you make a decision about how your child may function in kindergarten or early school years, you need some context in which to put his current pre-kindergarten achievements.

These activities are not intended to be one-sitting, one-hour tests. More likely one at a time will work best...just short spurts with no pressure, no big deal.

Auditory Functioning

When your child is in a good listening mood, tell him you want to play a listening game. Turn off any sound-making apparatus (no television or computer, no dishwasher, no radio, no nearby squabbling siblings). Ask him to turn on his ears, just as he would turn on the radio or TV. Do the motions with him.

Auditory: Evaluation 1

Words in a Sentence

Many children entering kindergarten can repeat a ten-word sentence. See how your child does with this. Of course you may change the sentences to match your child's interest. If you are a true grammarian, definitely change the eight-word and ten-word sentences.

Have your child repeat something you say, starting with a three-word sentence and then a four-word sentence, extending to longer sentences, such as:

Three-word: The dog barked.

Four-word: I want a drink.

Five-word: Is it my turn now?

Six-word: He threw the ball very hard.

Seven-word: I want to go outside and play.

Eight-word: Can I go to bed really late tonight?

Nine-word: May I have a cookie before I eat supper?

Ten-word: Can I buy a toy when we go out shopping?

Use some excitement in your voice when you say the words. If your child tires before you get to the ten-word sentence, discontinue. Resume another time, starting with the last number he repeated successfully in the previous try. Make it fun! It doesn't work if it isn't fun. And it doesn't work if he stops after sentence four to insist on a juice box. Hope for the best. It must be a game for him.

Auditory: Evaluation 2

Randomly Sequenced Lists

Have your child repeat after you a series of randomly sequenced items you say, starting with two, such as these numbers:

Two: 3–9
Three: 4–8–5
Four: 6–4–7–2
Five: 9–1–5–3–8
Six: 4–9–2–7–1–5
Seven: 8–6–3–1–5–9–4

Use animation in your voice and speak clearly. Don't go so fast that your child cannot separate the numbers, nor so slowly that he forgets in between. Be excited after each successful repetition. As your child progresses, tell him with mischievous daring, "It's going to get harder, are you ready?" It only works if he feels good about his performance. Whatever level he reaches, say something like, "You must be proud of yourself."

Many children entering kindergarten can repeat four units. Some can repeat five. A few can go to six. A very few can repeat all, or most, of seven units. Eight would be extraordinary.

You can change this game, using words. One syllable words of interest to your child make the best series.

Visual Functioning

The next level you may want to assess is your child's visual functioning ability. This is not the same as 20/20 physical eye capability, although a severe vision impairment may somewhat diminish his performance.

Find a relaxed, quiet time for both you and your child. A time when he isn't restless to play his new video game and you are not trying to squeeze in an activity before the washing machine finishes its cycle.

Visual: Evaluation 3

Reproducing Visual Units

Sit on the floor with your child, using some toy set he likes. If your child is playing with a farm set, for example, you isolate in front of him two different farm animals, perhaps a cow and a pig. After you put the two back with the others, ask your child to take out the two things you had put in front of him. If he can do two, next try three. Whenever he succeeds say something such as, "I can't fool you, can I?" Take turns with him; he'll love trying alternately to baffle you and amaze you.

Most kindergarten children can remember three visual units. When your child can do three, try for four. You know he's a genius, right?

This game can work with a variety of sets: blocks, cowboys, Barbie shoes, toy cars, etc. Your child also may have high interest with adult tools and hardware, make-up, jewelry.

Visual: Evaluation 4

Missing Visual Units

For another task, show your child three items (any three items familiar to him—a shoe, a book, a toothbrush, for example). While he turns his back, remove one of the items. When he turns back around, see if he can tell you which is now missing.

Next try four new items (any four—a block, a fork, a comb, a pencil, for example). Take away one; can he tell you which is no longer there?

Most kindergarten children can recall the one missing out of four visual units, providing the items are something they're familiar with and they are given a reasonable length of time to absorb. Too short a time doesn't allow recollection; too long a time brings indifference. Ten seconds is usually about right, but to establish your child's best time frame you may want to ask, "Are you ready to hide your eyes now?" or "Let me know when you're ready to turn around and not look."

Whenever he succeeds in naming the missing item, tell him something such as, "You really remembered!"

After he understands the system, alternate turns with him. See how far he can go with it. This visual memory game can be played many times in many places. When you're waiting in a doctor's office, for example, you can always pull something from your pocket or purse if nothing else is available. If you make it fun and not a burden, he'll want to do it frequently. He won't even realize you're making him smarter.

Visual: Evaluation 5

Ordering Visual Units

Most kindergarten-ready children know something about stoplights. They realize the red light is on top, the yellow light is in the middle, and the green light is on the bottom. Children can understand visual order when they see it, vertical or horizontal. They can tell you first, middle, last. (As proof, see if your child knows the difference between being first in line or last.)

For pre-kindergarten children, playing this game usually requires that the items you use be the same category. In other words, you may use a red block and a blue block and a yellow block of the same size and shape. Do not mix a red square block and a blue triangle block and a yellow arch block. You will want only one variable in this visual activity. To belabor the point, if you use different shape blocks, make them all the same color—a red square, a green square, a blue square. Colors do not have to be red, yellow, blue, but it helps to start with primary rather than exotic colors.

For simplicity, you can cut three circles out of paper: red, yellow, blue. Put them in a horizontal line:

Red   Yellow   Blue

We're beginning with circles because they require no special orientation to look like identical shapes. Give your child a few seconds to absorb this order. Do not say the color names, because that can introduce the element of auditory memory, and we're keeping here with visual functioning only. Pick up the three paper circles; mix their order. Hand the circles back to your child and have him put them in the same order you originally had them.

If your child does three units, see if he can do four; add a green, then purple, etc. If he's not precocious already, he will be if you continue like this. As always, if he's not having fun, *stop*!

Small Motor Skills

Because writing and drawing in some form is a part of any kindergarten, your child needs to have good eye-hand-muscle development and coordination. To help evaluate this, sit with him at a comfortable table level or desk. Put in front of him a clean sheet of paper and a pencil with an eraser. Be sure he is not distracted.

In evaluating your child's small motor ability, you will want to consider numerous things:

- Pencil hold
- Stroke pressure
- Time
- Ease of performance
- Starting and stopping points, direction
- Acceptable shape reproductions
- Position on the paper

1. The pencil is best held by thumb, index, and middle fingers, fairly near the point just above the sharpened exposed wood. Children who have not mastered this hold are more limited in their performance. Young children tend to display a high hold, giving them little strength or control in their strokes.

2. Some children use light, wispy strokes when writing. Others do a version of white knuckles, sometimes even breaking the pencil point with excessive pressure. A moderate stroke pressure is important for any lengthy school writing or drawing assignment.

3. Your child should draw these shapes in a reasonable time. Either extreme of excessively belaboring the task or dashing off a half-hearted attempt is less than desirable.

4. If your child agonizes, erases repeatedly or crosses out and restarts several times, discontinue the exercise. Obviously this is not fun.

Small Motor: Evaluation 6

Circles

Sit comfortably with paper and a pencil with an eraser. Begin by asking your child to draw a circle. Do not prompt, encourage, suggest, demonstrate, or correct.

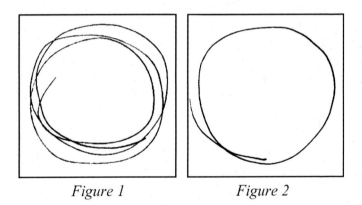

Figure 1   *Figure 2*

Figure 1–Young children start a circle at the bottom, move clockwise, and often continue circling.

Figure 2–As children mature, they may still overshoot, but they begin to limit their strokes.

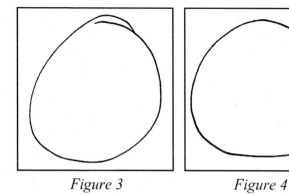

Figure 3   Figure 4

Figure 3–Eventually they start a circle at the top, perhaps still going clockwise and more oval.

Figure 4–Finally they start a circle at the top, moving counter-clockwise.

It is interesting to see that adults almost always start a circle at the top and move counter-clockwise. Left-handed writers can have variations that do not necessarily follow a developmental pattern.

While any of these above examples constitutes a circle, children ready for kindergarten usually have progressed at least to the stage represented in Figure 3, and often to Figure 4.

Small Motor: Evaluation 7

Drawing a Person

Sitting comfortably with your child at a table or desk, have paper and a pencil with an eraser. Pointing to a blank paper, tell your child you want him to draw a picture of a whole person. Do not prompt in any way, but do not rush his attempt. At minimum, pre-kindergarten children should be able to draw a stick figure. Children truly ready for kindergarten will include numerous parts of a person: head, eyes, nose, mouth, hair, arms, body, legs, feet. Some children draw very detailed and sophisticated people, including eyelashes, clothing, jewelry, fingers, and thumbs. Drawing additional items not asked for, such as a dog and a house and a tree, is not a plus. Following directions, "Draw a picture of a whole person," is more important for this evaluation than unsought creativity.

Often children's drawings follow this developmental pattern:

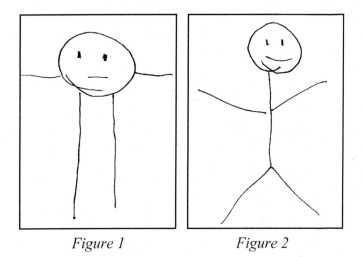

Figure 1   Figure 2

Figure 1–Children begin with the essence of a person.

Figure 2–The stick figure is a minimum drawing for school readiness.

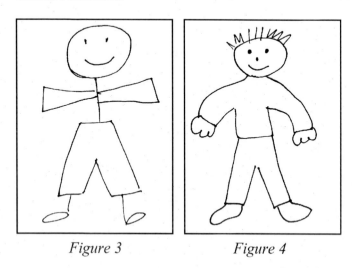

Figure 3   Figure 4

Figure 3–The stick figure becomes more dimensional.

Figure 4–The keen observer adds more features.

Figure 5   Figure 6

Figure 5–The most sophisticated are accurate with their elaborate inclusions and score the "most ready for school." If your child's work is on this level, it's a great performance.

Figure 6–Some children get carried away, which is not following the instructions and thus loses points for readiness, although the drawing is great. Your child may be a Rembrandt-in-the-making, but he gets no extra points here for artistic excellence or license. And Pollack splatters may earn $$$, but no kindergarten readiness points. This is small motor evaluation, not art evaluation.

Small Motor: Evaluation 8

Squares

At another time, sit comfortably with paper and pencil with an eraser. Tell your child you want to have some fun together. Begin by asking your child to draw a square.

Many children ready for kindergarten can draw a recognizable square. To qualify for this evaluation, a square needs to exhibit four corners. Sides do not need to be exactly equal in length, although extreme differences are not favorable.

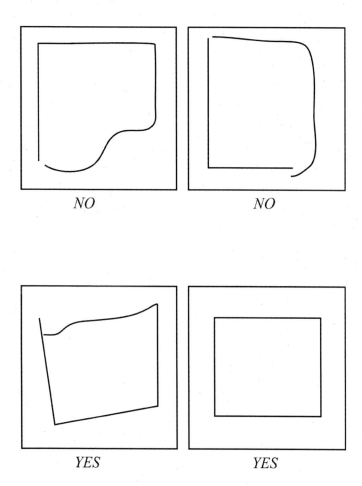

NO

NO

YES

YES

Small Motor: Evaluation 9

Triangles

At yet another time, sit comfortably with paper and pencil with an eraser. Begin by asking your child to draw a triangle.

A triangle is difficult for children to draw. While most children can make a capital A, fewer can envision dropping the cross line down to draw a triangle. If your child draws a triangle, that's great. To qualify, it must have three corner points.

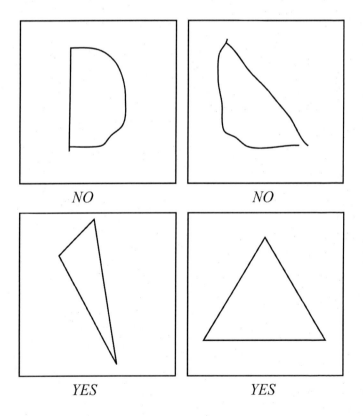

NO	*NO*
YES	*YES*

Small Motor: Evaluation 10

Position on the Paper

Sit comfortably at a table with your child, beginning with several sheets of paper and pencil with an eraser. Tell him you're going to have him draw some shapes. First ask him to draw a circle. When he finishes, ask him to draw a square. When that is done, have him draw a triangle.

Positioning of shapes on the paper gives you additional information about your child's small motor performance level. Do not prompt your child in any way. You can always teach him at another time. This is evaluation time, and you are evaluating his development, not your own.

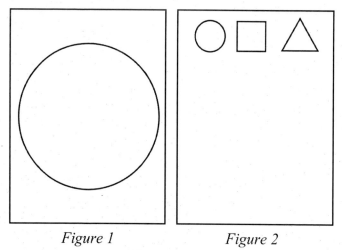

Figure 1   *Figure 2*

It is not unusual for a more immature child to follow the first direction on an epic scale, filling the entire page with his first assignment, not allowing space for any other entry (*Figure* 1). A more mature child will be apt to position his first instruction conservatively, anticipating there may be additional entries. If your child's work matches the second example here (*Figure* 2), that's quite advanced.

Letter Recognition and Reproduction

Most children have some letter recognition before kindergarten. This does not mean that you need to tutor your child immediately and intensely. Oh, *no*! But if your child has little interest in letters, on the McDonald's sign or at the stop sign or even in his name, he probably isn't tuned in yet.

Saying or singing the alphabet is a skill usually learned early on. This is rote memorization, promising no understanding of the use of letters. But it is a function often enjoyed by young children, and it does allow some pride in accomplishment. Furthermore, hearing and knowing letters by rote is an important first step in connecting the letters to written words.

Small Motor: Evaluation 11

Letters

Recognizing letters can take one of several forms. The simplest is pointing to a letter when asked to find it. Your child probably would enjoy any of several interactive computer games to learn letters. He would be even more excited if you would play with him, using the computer; and you could then assess his level.

Sitting in front of the computer with your child, use something like Arial font, 18 point, capitals. There are various ways to use this tool. He could type any letter at random and name that letter. You could type a letter and ask him to name it; he could type one and ask you to name it. If he cannot correctly name, he could type several letters and you could ask him to point to a letter that you name: "Can you point to the letter 'S'?" for example. Most children before they go to kindergarten can identify, by pointing when you say a letter name, to about ten to fifteen letters, using capital letters out of sequence; most can themselves correctly name about eight.

If he does well with capitals, try lower cases. Lowercase letters are somewhat harder for children because lowercase has more tricky similarities and height variances.

Some children can name all, or almost all, letters, tending to confuse most frequently the lowercase b,d,p; g,q; and v,w—those letters that look most alike.

We don't make letter identification easy for our children. There are many different letter symbols and systems, making it complicated for a child to decode: manuscript, circle and stick, D'Nealian, cursive, uppercase, and lowercase.

All of these are A's in some form:

A a *a* a ɑ *a* ɑ *A* ɑ A ℋ

The point is that **a** looks more like **d** than it looks like *a* or **A**. Go figure!

If your child is interested in letters on the computer, you two can choose a letter, large-sized font, and explore various font styles. It's quite an advanced exploration, so beware that you don't confuse him if he's not ready for this.

Printing his own name, or some recognizable form of his name, is important to a child. And when he starts kindergarten, it is very helpful for him to be able to recognize his name in print.

Number Counting, Understanding, Recognition, and Reproduction

Counting one through ten is easy for most pre-kindergarten children. As with reciting letters, this is rote memorization that does not assure any understanding of what numbers do, but it's the first step in learning about numbers. Many children can count into the pre-teens (eleven or twelve) and can recite the sequences starting with twenty-one, thirty-one, and forty-one. There are preschool children who can count to one hundred. Some children can count as long as an adult will listen. To be ready for kindergarten, your child should at least be counting to ten. After that, he may omit some numbers. But he should be proud of his work. Because there are fewer numbers, considering just one through ten, single numbers are easier than single letters, and number combinations (teens, etc.) are easier than letter combinations (cat, etc.).

Small Motor: Evaluation 12

Numbers

Sit with your child—comfortable chair, convenient time, casual setting—by now you know the drill. On a blank paper, you write number one. Ask your child, "Do you know what number this is?" Most kindergarten children recognize about half of the written numbers one through nine, and starting with one insures initial success. Then tell him, "I'm not going to write number two now, but can you tell me what number this is?" Then write four. If your child is able to say the numbers correctly, continue in some random order. Begin by writing only one number at a time to help him focus. If he is not able to do this successfully, write all the numbers at one time and ask your child if he can point to the number one, then the number two, number three. Sometimes pointing to a number you have named is easier than your child's having to say the number himself. If he is pointing, write the entire list at one time in some random order such as 1, 4, 8, 5, 2, 6, 3, 9, 7. Once again, using numbers on the computer might rouse your child's enthusiasm.

If your child seems to enjoy the numbers, you might ask if he wants to write some numbers himself. He may or may not be able to identify the number with its name.

Usually children can write and name two, three, or four numbers correctly and may attempt another one or two. It would be rare for a pre-kindergarten child to write double-digit numbers that he actually knows, more than writing any two random numbers. That is, most children could not write if you asked for a number such as forty-six; they would not connect those two numbers in their mind.

Cutting

Pre-kindergarten children often are fascinated by scissors. Almost every preschool child has cut his hair at least once, unauthorized but probably not unnoticed. A really scissors-enamored child also may go for the cat, his own shirt, and the drapes. Your child will attempt to cut only paper if you are lucky—and vigilant.

Small Motor: Evaluation 13

Cutting

Draw or print out computer copies of various shapes: a long single line, a square, a triangle, a circle, a wavy squiggle line. See how many your child can successfully cut. Most children can cut at least a single snip. Many can cut a straight line, using multiple snips. Therefore cutting a square is quite possible. While a triangle is the most difficult for a child to draw, it is within a child's ability to cut because it, too, uses only straight lines. A circle is the most difficult to cut because the arc requires continuous re-placement of the scissors angle. If your preschool child can cut a circle with reasonable accuracy, that is good small motor achievement. And it's most fun when children can cut squiggles; they many even enjoy drawing their own squiggles to cut.

Large Motor Skills

While not considered true academic readiness by some people, large motor skills are a valid and valuable asset, and a wonderful developmental tool not to be overlooked. These motor activities aid learning by increasing blood flow to the brain, easing tensions, and preparing the whole child for dealing with life.

Most children who enter kindergarten can balance on one foot for six to ten seconds, can walk backwards for ten steps, hop on one foot, bounce a ball, gallop, and skip.

A folksy evaluation is based on practices used in some world areas where birth records are not kept. To determine school readiness, a child puts his arm directly over the top of his head. If his hand can touch the opposite ear, he is school ready. While this may sound unscientific, it is based in the reality that an infant's head is proportionally larger than his body. In the first few years of life, the child's body grows to match head proportions. Thus, when the arm/hand can reach over the head to touch the ear, it's physical proof that he is now "ready." Whether you believe it or not, it's a touching practice.

> *Evaluating children for kindergarten readiness is something we do routinely in preschool. As you have been directed, we find a quiet place, quiet time, comfortable table—the optimum setting. As we take each child separately we say, "We're going to have some fun now; we're going to talk about kindergarten things." One dear five-year-old boy said, "Well, it's going to be a short talk, because I don't know much about kindergarten yet."*

These are the Norms and...

You have proved that you are extremely bright because you are reading this book. Therefore you probably know that your child is also extremely bright from the combination of your genes and your superior nurturing. But isn't it good to have your diagnosis confirmed by this second opinion?

With this information, you should now proceed either to "And what if he is" or "But what if he isn't." (Of course, you could benefit from reading both.)

AND WHAT IF HE IS

It's going to be an exciting ride for you!

Truly, you'll have fun exploring these activities. You may even learn new things along with your child. Remember, this is *not* a textbook; it's a way to enjoy the fullness of life.

The first thing you must do is permanently abandon the dread that your intelligent child might be bored.

Your child will absorb so much from everything going on around him. Be on your toes, though, because what you say and do, he will say and do (for better or worse). Isn't it startling when you hear his echo? Did you ever imagine that you sounded like that? Are you pleased?

Some days you may feel that you're playing "60 Questions in 60 Minutes." Bright children are curious. Parents of bright children have continuous opportunity to stimulate, inform, create, and most of all enjoy. Do be aware, however, that children do not always display brilliance across the board; often they have highs and lows. But for now we're celebrating, and we won't discuss the downside of that last sentence.

A search for knowledge is rather consistent among bright children; how each child searches for knowledge is not. Your child may have a long attention span, or he may flit. He may be quite vocal, or he may be the silent type, absorbing everything in preparation someday to write *The Great American Novel*. He may be impressively smart in math and science concepts, but show no evidence of genius in social savvy or emotional intelligence.

Overall then, you may define "being smart" in whatever way it best serves your child's needs. That definition does not have to correlate with anything else. Since you now have the power of Webster, this is what you do with it.

Start with Words

Be ready for any teachable moment. A teachable moment is when your child is listening to you (which may not happen often, so stay alert and at the ready).

Definitions and Functions

A teachable moment is when your child asks, "What does that mean?" or "What does this do?" A teachable moment is when you are riding in the car, having a meal together, just hangin,' getting him ready for bed. Use any teachable moment to discuss his comments and questions. By contrast, a teachable moment is *not* when he's tired and hungry, when he's glued to action video, or when he's thinking great thoughts (or something) that exclude you.

Rhyming

Hearing the actual sound of words is a great skill. Tell your child that some words rhyme, or sound alike. Show him that "cat" sounds like "sat," "rat," "mat," "hat," "bat." Make it animated, and only as long as your child is interested and having fun. Ask him if he can think of something that rhymes with:

1. cat (Even though you just told him, see if he understands—and help him be successful in the beginning.)

2. bat (or one of the other words he did not choose for 1.)

3. drink (If he doesn't get it, point to the sink; play charades if you must—blink, wink.)

4. floor (You may need to point to the door.)

5. chair (If necessary, point to your hair.)

6. moon (If he doesn't think of something on his own in a reasonable time, lay out a knife, a fork, and a spoon. See if he can get it then. If not, hold up the spoon.)

Many children four or five years old can grasp this concept. If your child can, it will be a fun game over and over—in the car, eating supper—instead of fighting with siblings. It's worth your effort to cultivate this skill. Your child, whether or not he has mastered the concept, might like giving you a word to see if you can rhyme. Children always like turning the tables, and who doesn't like to take control? Hopefully he won't throw you a curve with "orange" or "purple," but if he does, playfully explore with him non-words that rhyme; he'll surely giggle at "burple."

Speech

Motivation is everything. What child after watching *Mary Poppins* cannot say, "Supercalifragilistic?" Very young children quickly learn words to funny songs like "Magdelina Hagdelina who can walk 'em she can talk 'em hokum pocum nocum was her name." I assure you they can sing that.

Yet they may say "free" instead of "three" and "lellow" instead of "yellow." Have little concern if your child fails to say his y's; see if he can say "yucky." I told you, motivation is everything. And surely every garage sale adult you know can say "Three dollars" and not "Free dollars." Your child will learn, in good time. Normal pronunciation variances are normal in young children. Many children substitute these sounds:

W for R : one instead of run

L for Y : lellow instead of yellow

TH for S : thisther instead of sister

AH for R : foah instead of four

Regional accents can even reverse these mispronunciations. Southern charm might hold that a child should substitute WAH for R (example: fowah instead of four). St. Louis, on the other hand, may say farty instead of forty. Boston may say Americer.

And Chicago eats pizza with sassage. We'll leave that sanctioning to your discretion, and to your own dialect.

If there are sounds that your child makes incorrectly, even beyond regional pronunciations, it can help if you stress the sound when you say a word. When your child says, "The light is gween," you can offer, "Yes, the light is grrreen." Stress the rrr … without sounding ridiculous, but do stress it. Again, he certainly can "grrrrrrowl" like a tiger.

In extreme circumstances, you may want to consult a speech expert, one who understands and specializes in working with preschool children. This may be necessary if your child's speech variations make him unable to communicate with other children, and therefore he becomes embarrassed and withdrawn.

In any event, your child may enjoy playing this game with you. Say a long word, or a pretend word, or a silly word, and have your child say it after you. You may want to start with:

- Giggle bug
- Humdinger
- Noodle doodle
- Jelly roll belly roll
- Big boo boo
- Big boo hoo hoo (you may act here as though you are crying)

Use whatever words or non-words you choose. Get as silly as you like. Your child may delight in making up his own words which you then repeat; take turns. By this time you should both be doubled over with laughter. Caution: your child may want to play this game again and again, perhaps even in front of other adults. We'll leave it to you to do the explaining.

If presented properly, word games are great articulation exercises for children. Your child should have so much fun that he doesn't realize you're expanding his verbal intelligence.

Vocabulary

When your child has developed a love for words, you can try real words that do have meaning. He may even ask what some of these big words mean as you say them. This works best in conversation; don't try a list of them run together. While natural opportunity is best, you may want to include:

- Frustrated

- Inspired

- Famished

- Delighted

- Unaware

- Perplexed

- Ridiculous

- Befuddled (College Dictionary, page 47)

- Bedfellow (Is his dog a bedfellow?)

Your child may astound you with his increasing vocabulary. And these are all words he can appropriately, even proudly, use in front of Grandma.

Opposites and Categories

Explore with him words that mean the opposite. Hot and cold, wet and dry, happy and sad. If he's good at this, and you may play it often, try finding a gradation word that is somewhere inbetween. Hot and cold can be warm; wet and dry can be moist. And what about happy and sad—doesn't that open the door for interesting discussion of words and feelings. Be prepared for him to ask you the opposite of drapes or broccoli. This gives you great opportunity to have fun with language.

Try categories. Transportation: cars, boats, rockets, etc. Colors, fruits, relatives. It's fun to take turns with everyone in the group, but if siblings are at an age disadvantage, they may need to be on a team with an adult. The objective is to explore and enjoy the concepts of words. Play the game in a way that affirms every child, and makes you look good too.

Extending the understanding of categories, discuss how things are alike and/or different: hat, coat, gloves; happy, sad, angry; fire truck, stop sign, clown's nose. (Do you need to think about that last one?)

Talk about what does not belong and why in a list of words: apple, banana, orange, green beans; or a different combination of green beans, lettuce, peas, carrots, limes.

The goal of these word games is not so much to be correct as it is to open your child's mind by stimulating his awareness, refining his thinking process, increasing his precision thinking skills.

Reasoning

Talk with your child about the world. Where do things come from: milk, metal, water, paper, carrots, ice cubes? Who makes things: cars, plastic, keys, bread, toys? How do they work: washing machine, freezer, pencil sharpener, music box? What are they used for: thermometer, ruler, scales, boat, car, airplane? What would happen if: the car ran out of gas, the lamp were unplugged, we didn't have windows in our house, all food tasted like brussel sprouts or chocolate chip cookies? You are allowed, perhaps even encouraged, to consult outside resources and other authorities before bringing up these topics.

Move on to Reading

If your child is interested in reading, *read read read* with him. After all, it may be your only chance to sit and relax from now until he goes off to college.

Smart children usually want, in addition to having a book read to them, to know what individual words "say." Take your finger, or your child's, and point to words as you read them. Don't worry that this will cause his reading to be stilted. When he becomes more proficient in reading, pointing will serve no purpose and will disappear. For now, it's enough to have him realize that a particular group of letters makes a word he can say aloud.

Retelling and Comprehension

After you have read a book to your child, ask him to retell that story. Listen for correct sequence. If he hesitates, suggest, "What did she do after that?" Give more hints if necessary.

As your child retells an interesting event from the story, ask questions for comprehension. Why do you think she did that? How can you tell the girl was sad? Why was the boy angry? How many pancakes did the girl eat?

Creative Thinking

Discuss other possibilities: What if Cinderella had not gone to the ball? What if she had left earlier and her glass slipper had not fallen off? How would the Prince have found her? What would her stepsisters have said if her beautiful dress had turned back into rags while she was still dancing at the ball? And what would the Prince have done? Have your child give reasons for his opinions about the stories.

Comparing and Contrasting

The next stage in reading is having your intelligent child compare and contrast two stories you have just read. How were Sleeping Beauty and Snow White alike? Think of as many ways as you can. Then, How were they different?

Now Your Child Becomes an Author

Planning

For a final stage of reading, help your child write his own stories. Have a book form made up in advance; papers stapled together will do, but loose sheets of paper are not as impressive. Some stores or children's catalogues sell blank books for children's writing, about four heavy pages folded and stapled in the middle. Whatever you use, it should look like a book just waiting for his words.

Developing a Plot

Your child will be the author, but you may need to be the prompter. Help him keep some continuity, which is more important here than letting him wander in aimless, disjointed creativity. Save stream of consciousness writing for college courses.

The prompter begins by asking what the child wants to write about—people, animals, what? Start with general categories, then narrow down. If he says people, ask: a real person, a girl, a boy, a pretend person, what do you think? Keep narrowing and defining: how old is this boy? What is his name? Where does he live? Is he nice? What does he do? Is there anyone else in the story?

Help your child/author develop a plot. Say with great interest, "Then what did he do? What did he think about that? How did that happen?"

Putting It on Paper

As your child dictates, you write. If your child likes to draw, leave space on each page for him to illustrate. If he can and wants to print some or all of the words, encourage that. You may even want to print key words for him to copy when you come to that place in the story. He may be more eager to print a dramatic word than easier, common words such as "the." You can at least encourage his printing an exciting word or two; if he's mastered and is proud of printing "the," what a great opportunity. It also will give him pride in his proprietary interest; you printed 108 words, he printed one, it's his printing—children's law. Progressively he may want to write more words, even with his personal creative spelling. Eventually he will write it all himself.

If your child thrives as a writer, you may even opt to have one of his books published using a commercial kit that produces a professional finished product for children.

Deciding on a Title

Your prompting guides him to decide the characters, establish a plot, and reach a conclusion (the denouement, usually known in children's books as a happy ending). Then your child chooses a title. If he has difficulty, ask him what his story is about. This can help him see what a good title might be.

Making a Cover

When the book is finished, make a nice cover with perhaps a colored tape binding. Your child can draw a picture on the cover. You or he can write the title, but it's necessary that he have at least some hand in this.

Finding a Proper Display Site

Then he places it on the family bookshelf, or on the living room coffee table, in some very prominent place. It should be read frequently and treated with great respect always.

Usually this will result in a child's wanting to write another and another. With good luck, he will become a best-selling author and provide posh care for you in your dotage. With certainty, he will become a lifelong lover of books.

Spelling and Writing

Writing, for children, includes any attempt to put pencil to paper. If your child has good pencil control and if he likes drawing and/or writing, supply him with black pencils and colored pencils and washable markers and crayons, lots of different kinds and colors of paper, and a convenient place to store and use them all. Since you have mastered the solution to "But He's Messing up the House," he will of course store them properly in an accommodating place you have provided.

Printing

When your child is interested in printing letters, sit with him. Each of you should have your own paper and pencil. Ask what letter he would like to make, perhaps discussing the sound that letter makes and a few words that begin with that sound. (Most letters have the same sound in most words, but a few, especially vowels, can sound different. For example, "a" may say angel or apple. If your child is confused by that, you can tell him it's one of those letters that tries to trick him.) He may, for example, choose "s." You can both think of "s" words—snake, silly, sleepy, stop. You make an "s" and then have him write an "s." Next it's your turn to choose a letter and his turn to print first. If he has difficulty printing letters, you continue to print and let him copy.

If your child is very advanced and can write most letters, he may be interested in matching uppercase/capital letters to lowercase letters, and D'Nealian with manuscript. In the off chance that you haven't taught first grade recently, you can find samples of these on the computer. (You may want to call your child's future grade school directly to ask what alphabet system they use for writing; alphabet styles of choice can change from one year to the next.) Any font can provide capital and lowercase and the Internet can give complete alphabets in the various printing systems. Your child will be amazed at how intelligent you are. Dazzle him while you can.

Using Mail

Writing and mailing letters, and getting something back, gives your child a great sense of power. Help him write a note to Granddad, to Santa, to someone who will write back; teach him the good manners of writing a thank you note. He doesn't need to print all the words himself; printing several words will give him ownership. How powerful it is to evoke a written response. Just be sure the person to whom he will be writing will reliably reply. It's even better if Granddad includes a sticker or something super.

The most impressive is if he can help you order something for him in writing. What bright child wouldn't be eager to write the name of Tonka on an order blank and have it sent to him? And to write your credit card numbers? Check to be certain that he writes under quantity: "1" and not "10."

He may also delight in writing and receiving e-mail. That, of course, requires close monitoring for safety and security, and/or an in-house techie person who can master blocking.

Visual Perception Exercises

Play "I Can Do This, I Can Do That" with your child. Find your comfortable writing area, each of you sitting with a sheet of paper and a writing tool. You start by drawing or writing some squiggle or shape on your paper, saying, "I can do this." Your child replies, "I can do that," and draws or writes the same thing that you did. Then he adds something, saying, "I can do this." To which you reply, "I can do that," and do. This does not have to "make" anything; it's just doodling on a page. But it helps your child's visual acuity.

Visual perception is also stimulated by determining figure orientation. Draw for your child a triangle with the point on top and a triangle with the point on the bottom. Show him the two. Then draw aside a separate triangle with the point on top and ask him which one it matches. Next print a capital M and a capital W. Print a separate W and see if he can pick out the letter it matches. If he enjoys this activity, he may delight in making his own images with the computer, using some exotic fonts such as Symbol or Wingdings.

Art

Two categories of art are explored in this section: drawing creations and fine art appreciation. If artistic creations are your "thing," you may also rush out to buy modeling clays and wood burning sets. Go nuts!

Mystery Drawing

Sit with your child for a mystery drawing game. Give him an unlined sheet of paper and a pencil. Tell him you're going to give him instructions and see how soon he can discover what he's drawing. Tell him to:

- Draw one large circle near the bottom of the page.

- Draw a little smaller circle above the large circle and make it touch the top of the circle he's just drawn.

- Draw a third circle smaller than the last circle he just made, and make it touch the top of the last circle he drew.

- Draw a hat on top of the smallest circle.

- Draw a face and arms on the snowman (which by now he has identified, unless perhaps you live at the Equator).

If your child enjoys drawing, he may be inspired by books that teach step-by-step shapes resulting in an animal, person, or thing. He'll be awed if you study the book first and teach him.

Concepts

Start with two identical square pieces of paper. Tell your child, "I'm going to do something with this paper. I want you to watch, and when I'm through I want you to do the same thing." Fold your square diagonally to make a triangle (*Figure* 1), then put the end points together and fold again, making a smaller triangle (*Figure* 2). Say, "Can you do the same thing?" Can he?

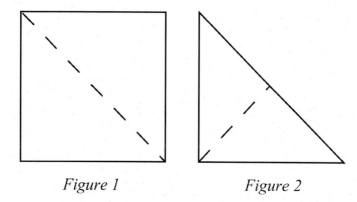

| Figure 1 | Figure 2 |

Can he tell you how a circle is like the top of a glass, or a rectangle like a piece of paper and like a door? It's exciting when a child begins to make conceptual comparisons.

Colors

If your child has an artistic interest in color and shadings, get long color strips from a paint or hardware store, two of each strip. Start with one color, perhaps red, cutting one strip into individual color sections and keeping the other intact. See if you and your child can match the individual shades with the whole strip. If your intelligent child is so intelligent that he matches the numbers, cut them off and write them on the back of the individual shades. Some days you need to outsmart your smart offspring. These colors can be kept in individual baggies for repeated play. As your child's skill increases, you can use more-and-more similar hues.

Museum and Fine Art

On trips to the library, show your child pictures of drawings by Monet for beautiful use of colors and by Picasso for creativity. Some libraries even have museum quality art that you can take home (reproductions only, of course), like checking out books. Keep a hook ready and exchange free fine art pictures regularly. Because it's temporary, you don't even have to color coordinate to fit the decorating scheme of your child's room.

Through the Internet, you can access wonderful pictures of the masters and moderns. You and your child can search for pictures that look as real as if taken by a camera, or so abstract you can only speculate what it is. Art sales companies list their products by artists, by categories, by colors, by sizes, by content, etc. Be sure to explore and inspire your child's interest in fine art. It will be a lifetime gift from you to him.

There are books featuring pictures of fine art that include a common feature: on each page can you spot the dog, for example. This is far more toney than common books with hidden objects, and it teaches far more. Art exploration can teach your child to be a keen observer. He may even be able to find his socks and pajamas someday—or maybe not.

Displays

Displaying your child's writing and drawing can give him great pride in his work. But have you been in homes where you can't find the refrigerator because it's hiding behind the art displays? Should it become a choice between feeding your child's mind and feeding his stomach, you know what has to be eliminated.

If your child wants to display in your home every paper he ever completed, you, too, may need to get creative. Find a display spot, devoted exclusively to his work. You can feature a masterpiece of the day or of the week, changing the display (but probably not permanently discarding anything he ever created). Or you can do layers, as some galleries do. This can be accomplished by hanging two hooks, and then punching two holes in each masterpiece to hang on the hooks, or one hook and one hole strung on a loop. You also could make a display box to house the masterpieces upright for review, as you see in an art store selling pictures. If you are extraordinarily artistic yourself, you may be able to mount and display his work on the walls of your home. Colored construction paper or wallpaper (expired books free from stores) can make an inexpensive mounting feature. If your creative child inherited his creativity from you, you can conquer this.

Music

A simple concept for children to understand is that there are four basic ways to make music:

- With your mouth as in singing, humming, whistling, clicking your tongue

- By blowing or pushing air through something such as a horn, harmonica, accordion, organ

- By tapping, hitting, pounding things such as drums, piano, organ, xylophone; shaking things such as bells, castanets, tambourine

- By strumming such instruments as guitar, harp, violin, lyre

Your child may be enamored of the many room-shaking electronic capabilities, but we won't speak of that here. All in good time, you can surrender to his volume frenzy, but that's for a later day.

Music is a joy of its own, but it is also connected to the ability to process language, math, and science functions. Use it with your child. (Note: This obviously is not a recommendation for acid rock or junk. We're pushing creativity here, not destruction.)

Movement to music is natural for children. You can intensify this expression with twirling scarves, pompons, batons, whatever props add to your child's creative dance expression.

For young children, elements of music are rhythms, tones, and words. More advanced musical awareness can identify differences in musical instruments, but that is really sophisticated.

Rhythms

Children love rhythms, and the ability to "keep time to the beat of music" is developed when children are very young. Even babies as they are rocked and lullabied and patted can absorb rhythm.

Rhythms begin with patterns. Make a pattern by clapping your hands or tapping your feet. Begin with a simple *clap-clap-clap*, then try *clap-clap-pause-clap*. If your child can reproduce that, make your pattern more complex. Take turns with your child initiating or following a pattern. This is a great activity at the kitchen table. The whole family can be involved. Children especially like to tap their hands under the table, unseen. You can drum on oatmeal boxes or coffee cans, but do make rhythms. Be creative.

Beginning to Read Music

To help your child realize that rhythms are music, you can make lines (a forerunner to notes) on a page. Begin by running your finger along a solid line,

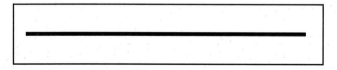

Singing Laaaaaaaaaa the entire time.

The spacing of lines can show when to sing, "*Laaa.*" Run a finger along the page, singing only when there is a line and pausing when there is a blank. You may need to put your finger to your lips and say, "Shhh," for your child to master the concept of the quiet time. Begin with even rhythms, pointing to the chart.

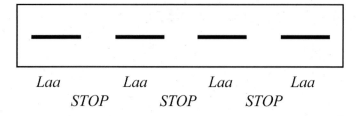

Laa   *Laa*   *Laa*   *Laa*
     STOP   *STOP*   *STOP*

Then use uneven rhythms.

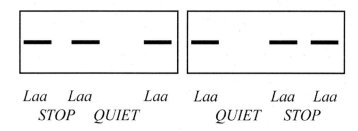

Laa   *Laa*   *Laa*   *Laa*   *Laa*   *Laa*
   STOP   *QUIET*   *QUIET*   *STOP*

To encourage development of tonal cognizance, sing a low note and then a high note for your child. (Just sing however you can. *Laaa.* This is not your audition for Three Tenors or the Met. And the most wonderful thing about children is they love you anyway. Usually…) Ask him to tell you whether the first was lower or higher than the second. Progressively diminish the distance between the two, until they are just a note or two apart. See how keenly your child can distinguish tones. Also give your child a chance to sing notes to you. If he can readily distinguish higher or lower pitch between two notes, try three to see if he can identify the lowest or the highest. In addition to singing *Laaa*, vary by singing other sounds such as *Ahhh, Oooo, Eeee*, whatever.

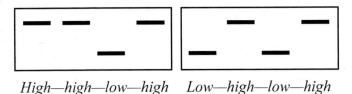

High—high—low—high   Low—high—low—high

Be sure to stop, not glide, when there is no line.

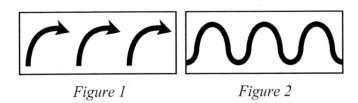

Figure 1   *Figure 2*

Figure 1–Start as low as you can and glide up, up, up. Turn it upside down and glide high to low.

Figure 2–Make this one sound like a siren. Here's hoping you like it, because your child will want to sing it again and again.

Tones

The sounds of music can seem mysterious to children. To make music more tangible for your curious child, you can try two things. In the first experiment, set out several identical glasses. They should be transparent, real glass, and cheap. No fine crystal here; your child may have to wait two more decades for that experiment. Line the glasses in a row and fill them with varying amounts of water. Then take a spoon and tap the side of each glass to make a musical sound. Discuss with your child how the sounds are different. Does more water make the sounds higher or lower? What if the glasses are not identical? If you add food coloring, would the color make any difference? What if you added a drop or two of vegetable oil? Or salt? This visual connection to sound can make music much more tangible for your child. If you work on this, your child could develop enough musical talent, a.k.a. understanding, to play a simple song.

A second experiment to give your child understanding and control of music requires a box and several different sized rubber bands. A shoebox is ideal. String the rubber bands around the open box and strum with fingers or a variety of picks (pencil, spoon, paper clip). Discuss how the rubber band determines the pitch or the sound. Does a shorter or longer rubber band make the higher sound? What about narrower or wider?

Now you have a two-piece band. Your child on the glasses and you on the rubber band shoebox. Could anything else strip you of your dignity so quickly and yet keep you smiling as you perform?

If your child still likes this foray into music, you can make other rhythm or note pattern cards. And if he's really musically smart, he may enjoy your combining on a card both the rhythm and tone elements. Thus you would sing *laaa* and he could write rhythms for you both explore. Any lines, high or low on the page; straight, curved, or angled; long or short can be interpreted. He can begin pre-composition of music.

Be creative, and encourage your child to be creative.

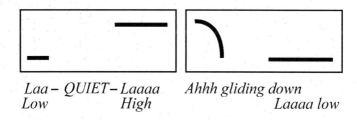

Laa – QUIET– Laaaa   *Ahhh gliding down*
Low   High   *Laaaa low*

Then you can changes lines to notes on a staff.

Five lines, a treble clef sign, and notes wherever you and your child choose to put them. If you're a gifted musician, you can be as precise as your child finds interesting. You can tell him when he sees the five lines, he may think he's going to write letters and words. But when he sees the clef sign, he knows it's music. He can make his song go up, down, or stay the same. The timing of notes, long or short, is probably too complex for your child to enjoy…but who knows, he may be a musical genius.

Soon you may need join ASCAP. But first you have to tackle the words. You can make rhythms with your voice: cadence, hip-hop, chants, rhyming lines, poems, echoing (in which the second person repeats what the first said, using the same rhythm). Next put the rhythmic words to music. Rhythms can be extended to marching and dancing. Feel the beat?

For bright children, phonics songs bring together all the elements of music, language, and math. You can download clever (and free) phonic songs and pictures on our Web site: www.childexcel.com. For example, you and your child can laugh at the poem/song about a flea and a fly who had the flu, and you'll love the illustrations. Discover rhyming words as well as words that start with the letter F.

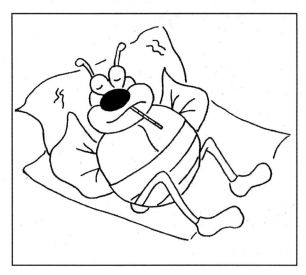

A flea and a fly had the flu.
Their fever was one-fifty-two.
The flea held his head and the fly flew to bed
For they felt very frail, wouldn't you?

Some young children understand the concept of alliteration. Many enjoy the sound repetitions without realizing they are learning phonics.

Composing

The most sophisticated development is when your child begins to create his own music. Many children make sporadic playful attempts, and that is never to be discouraged. But if he is interested, he can create a more formal composition and thus feel a real sense of achievement. Again you assume the role of prompter, and he is the composer. Similar to writing the book, begin by asking your child what he would like to write a song about, etc.

You must write down at least the words he dictates. In this case, you do need to arrive at a somewhat rhythmic and poetic four-liner. If he finishes a line but has trouble finding a rhyming word to end the next line, help him explore. For example, if the first line is, "I love to drive my car," then you begin with the alphabet in an attempt to find a rhyming word: are, bar, dar, far, etc. It's fun to eliminate the words that are not real words, and it's a learning experience for him to discover words he never knew. So he may connect, "I love to drive my car;

I drive it very far." Once he masters this system, he can truly take off.

If you also can write his notes, or coordinate with a piano or other musical instrument, do so. Otherwise, remember the tune and try to find a friend who will write down the musical notes on a score. If even that is not a practical option, above his written words just make a staff (five lines) and some musical notes, whether or not they correspond identically to your child's tune. Try to have your written notes go up when his go up, and down when his song goes down. Absolute accuracy is not absolutely necessary at this level. After all, Chopin in his current state cannot critique it.

Recording

Make a tape/CD/DVD of his song, audio or video, and he can play it whenever he wants. Give a copy to grandparents or to very, very good friends. Photostat copies of his song and use them for group singing—around the dinner table, when grandparents visit, or whenever you can garner a volunteer or two (those who made the cut and listened to/watched the tape/CD/DVD). This may reveal who your true friends are.

Your child will probably delight in giving a "show" if you'll watch with rapt and affirming attention. If you're truly into this, someone can videotape his entire show. Once your child has become a star, you may be able to blackmail him with this early effort. Your possibility of blackmail diminishes in opposite correlation with your expertise as his music teacher.

A love of music can enrich a life forever. Give your child that advantage...and you'll enjoy it yourself.

Math

While many children can count by rote memory, it's exciting when a child can put a concept, or the understanding of concrete meaning, to the number.

Concepts

Lay out four spoons and ask your child how many are there. Have him add another spoon and tell you how many are there. Take away two and ask him how many are there. This is the principle for understanding numbers. Use this in a variety of ways (different items such as pennies, toothpicks, etc.). Try various math processes. Addition: two pennies added to four pennies gives you six. Subtraction: six toothpicks, taking away one, leaves five.

Graphs

Bright children especially enjoy working with graphs. Draw a grid with four or five squares across and several squares down. M&Ms are wonderful for this process. Give your child a few of each color and have him vertically line all the reds in one column, all the browns in another, etc. For the beginning grapher, it's most meaningful if the items can be physically moved about.

Red	Yellow	Brown	Green
O	O	O	O
O	O	O	
		O	
		O	

When he is finished laying out the colors, let him decide which column has the most and which has the least. He can do many experiments with this. How many more greens would he need to have as many as the reds? If he added together the two reds and the two yellows, would that be as many as the browns? How many yellows would he need to make the same number as the browns on the graph? You get the picture: reds + yellows + greens = more than browns. If it is helpful, he can, for example, move the reds and yellows into the same column to see that they together equal the number of browns. If he counts them: reds + yellows = 4; browns are 4; they're the same number.

You can graph preferences. If you have only two choices on your graph, you would have only two vertical columns and as many horizontal columns as people you ask. For example, who prefers chocolate or vanilla ice cream:

Chocolate	Vanilla
Grandma	Daddy
Carlene	Mother
Aunt Beth	Uncle Phil
Mrs. Jones	Josh
The mailman	The babysitter

Do more people prefer chocolate or vanilla? Your child may want to write names or titles on small pieces of paper and move them around—do more men or women like chocolate, for example.

Patterns

Patterns are intriguing to bright children. The simplest kinds are A B A B A, what comes next? Cutouts of red, yellow, green, red, yellow, green, red...? Very bright children can discern amazingly elusive patterns and puzzles. You can use symbols from computer fonts or just write/draw your own. For example, draw shapes:

Circle Triangle Circle Triangle Circle ?

Then you and your child can take turns making your own correlating patterns:

There could be more than one answer to patterns too. You can buy books with patterns, or you can design your own.

Patterning can become coding, which is exciting for children. Every letter can have a symbol: another letter, a number, a shape. Only you and your child have the master code, so only the two of you can decode messages: # stands for A, @ stands for B, * stands for C, and so on; whatever you and your child decide.

With a code, you can write secret messages to each other. Your child will especially love it if you write something like, "Let's read." Initially make the messages short, for obvious reasons.

Multiplication

Put your hand in the silverware drawer two times and take out two spoons each time. How many spoons do you have? Yes, two times two equals four. Put your hand in the drawer two times and take out nothing each time. Two times zero (nothing) is zero (nothing).

Have your child put his hand in a bag of candy three times and take out one piece each time. So how much is three times one?

How many people are sitting at your dinner table? Perhaps there are four people, each with two hands. Each person should lay his hands on the table. Count how many hands there are altogether. Four people with two hands makes eight hands. Each person also has two feet under the table. Guess how many feet there would be.

Algebra

The next concept involves beginning algebraic procedures, and can be readily enjoyed by a bright child. This should not be presented to your child until he understands the concepts of simple addition and subtraction. Understanding does not require a correct numerical answer each time, but does require comprehension of the basic process. Start with two apples and one banana. Add two bananas. Now you have two apples and three bananas (2 apples + 1 banana + 2 bananas = 2 apples + 3 bananas; or 2 A + 1 B + 2 B = 2 A + 3 B) or five pieces of fruit (5AB). Simple, basic algebra. You would not expect your child to master or even wrestle with a written formula, but this concept is meaningful to a child interested in numbers and sets. If it would help, actually have apples and bananas (or something else) to move about and count; you could even write on/post-it-note/label the items to make it more concrete for your child to understand. Once he gets the concept, it's his forever.

The point of these games is not to teach your child algebra and multiplication tables before anyone else his age, but to help him make the connection between numbers and the concrete real world they represent.

Science

Science is a valuable component for your child's intellectual development. The scientific process uses inductive or deductive reasoning. Inductive reasoning predicts what might happen; deductive reasoning tries to determine what is true. I'm not suggesting that you get a PhD in science and try to explain the difference between inductive and deductive reasoning to your child. But using these procedures can start your child on a good path to precision thinking.

Inductive reasoning starts with some things you already know to be true and leads you to predict what will happen or what will be. For a fun experiment, sit with your child at a table with an unopened Hershey bar (or some tidbit that might be his favorite) in front of you. Discuss what he already knows about Hershey bars:

- Every Hershey bar he has ever eaten was sweet.

- Every Hershey bar he has ever eaten was chocolate and it melted in his hand if he held it too long, etc.

Knowing this, what can he predict, what does he expect, about the new bar? Open the new Hershey and see if those predictions are right. What would he predict, or expect, about every other Hershey bar? You don't have to use sophisticated words about this scientific thought process, but what child wouldn't be interested in an experiment with candy? If you wanted to get really precise, you could have a Hershey bar that is bittersweet chocolate, or milk chocolate with almonds, etc. The purpose of this would be not to confuse, but to show that there can be even more information that you didn't consider the first time.

Inductive reasoning is the basis of common sense. The stoplight changed from green to yellow to red in his previous experience; it will probably change from green to yellow to red this time.

Deductive reasoning begins with generalizations and draws a conclusion. This time for an experiment, put M&Ms in a bag and do not let your child see them. Discuss with your child:

- We know that all Hershey bars are sweet.
- The candy in this bag is sweet.

Knowing this, can you be sure the candy in this bag is a Hershey bar? Look in the bag. Oops! What went wrong? He didn't have all the information. Hershey bars are rectangles; this candy is round. As you gather more information or generalizations, you move toward good deductive reasoning. If he had shaken the bag, he would have heard a sound different from a Hershey bar. Had he seen the shapes and colors, he would have known it was not a Hershey bar. This can demonstrate to a curious mind how important it is to include all the facts. It can help a bright child to wonder, "Is there something else I need to know?"

In Conclusion

If your child has been blessed with great intelligence, it's a wondrous thing. You can develop it, nurture it, mold it. More important, you can help your child make that intelligence effective. Scattered intelligence without purpose or self-control is a terrible loss.

Do not be inundated with pages and pages of suggested activities. They're much easier than they seem at first glance. Take one thing at a time, try it, have fun with it, see if your child is interested.

When you talk with your intelligent child, help him to stay on topic. Do not confuse creativity with aimlessness. Mental wandering has its necessary time and productive place, but it is not a substitute for clear thinking.

Please note that in all the suggestions for helping your intelligent child, you did not find any directions such as use flashcards, make him sit alone and do his numbers and letters, keep him at the computer until he reaches the final challenge, concentrate on academics so he'll be ready for kindergarten, or be sure he can read by the time he's four.

BUT WHAT IF HE ISN'T

You know that children develop at different rates. A child who is underweight for his age and height at two years old may grow, literally, to be an NFL linebacker. Who knew? The ugly ducking story, the tortoise and the hare, the school drop-out turned computer expert bizillionaire. Unlikely success stories abound. Who knew...you will. Muscles and brains need time for biological development. And just as there are body growth spurts, there are brain spurts. You know that children change, and that you have the power to help your child change—to help him grow in the direction you lead.

Of course there are late bloomers, and with luck, your child (and all children) will continue to bloom until he is at least one hundred years old. But let this be a warning: be careful what you wish for. Sometimes when you nurture the bloom, it really blossoms beyond your dreams. As one example, a very shy child can blossom into a child who is always center stage. So in your best interest, we will flag this *"Blooming Alert!"* sign in any area where your child may well have a huge, unexpected spurt.

Think of this as a conversion chapter. Nothing is more exciting than making a problem situation into a success story, especially for your own child.

This chapter shows you how to do just that.

Plan for Success

If your child is not academically or developmentally where you would like him to be, let's talk.

First, there are necessary rules, not for your child, but for you.

- Know that you can do miracles—you really can.

- Use your observation, your intuition, your creativity, and your love to make these things happen.

- Be informed—and this book will help.

- Make it fun.

Success is particularly important for an underachieving child; failure is a setback. Give your child an environment for success. Never let your child think or say, "I can't do it." Of course there are things he cannot do—everyone has things he cannot do—but he can say, "I haven't done it yet."

Games

Play games that are cooperative, not competitive. Encourage team play in your home whenever you can. For example, linger at the dinner table after the meal is eaten. Play any of the word games in from the previous chapter, with this adaptation. Have Mom and child on one team, and Dad (with or without other children) on another, whatever fits your table attendance. If you were doing a categories game, you would use this opportunity to discuss among your teammates "what does not belong" or "how are they alike" and come up with a group answer. Every discussion gives your child a built-in success. Your family structure may be different, your games may be different, but the learning opportunity is the same. Instead of "I won," which automatically implies someone else lost, the result is "We did it!"

For activities such as board games, when one player reaches the goal (the pot of gold, the palace, the end, whatever), the game is over. There doesn't have to be a declared winner, the game is just over. If your losing child finds satisfaction in completing his game after someone else has already finished, that's great too. But a winner need not be declared. Everybody played, everybody finished. What fun.

Encouragement

Words of encouragement are important to an underachiever. In this case, don't worry about the praise junkie syndrome. You have a different, more pressing, agenda. Make a list of the encouraging words that best motivate and inspire your child:

> That's the way to do it!
> Wow!
> Now you've figured it out!
> I knew you could do it!
> You're learning fast!
> That's *it*!
> Let's call Dad at work and tell him.
> You're getting better every day!

That's the way!
Way to go!
Good thinking.
That's what I call a fine job.
You've just about mastered it.
I think you've been practicing.
You're really improving!
You'll have to show Grandma!
You make it look easy.
How did you do that?
Much better!
You should be proud of yourself!

Use them whenever your child's effort justifies encouragement.

Gratification

Feel free to reward your child for his accomplishments; disregard any guilt for your bribery (which it really isn't). Call it a "celebration of success," and have many. He accurately counted to twenty for the first time, let him then count and eat twenty raisins (or do something else he likes in an increment of twenty). He counted four forks, knives, and spoons for the dinner table, give him an extra scoop of dessert ice cream, or four minutes of his talking to the family without interruption, or an extra four minutes before bedtime. He wrote his name correctly for the first time, give him three cheers (yeah Johnny, yeah Johnny, yeah Johnny). For variation, give a silent cheer with arms raised and fists pulsing upward and a face that mimes yeahhh! The silent cheer can be useful whenever you want to celebrate without making a spectacle, such as when you're out in public. It also can help lower the decibels during any celebration. He tried really hard to accomplish something, give him "huge hungry hugs" where you hug and kiss his neck and laugh—hereafter known as gimmie some, or here's a'comin, some HHH. By the way, this book does not guarantee that your child will look forward to HHH, so you may have to find another acknowledgment activity.

Positive Teaching Methods

When your child is not a high achiever, it is especially important that you "teach by teaching and not by correcting." Disregard advice to correct errors on the spot. You don't need to tell him he's wrong; he may realize that all too often. For example, if your child pushes his chair into the table, dragging it on the floor and making a lot of noise and bumping the table, do not address it then. Wait a bit, then say, "Let me show you something." Then you can demonstrate lifting the chair, and both of you can do this activity several times. If the situation must be addressed at the moment of action, the most you should say is, "Let me show you another way (or a different way) to do that." When you teach by teaching, you do not diminish your child's self-image.

"I" Messages—the Wrong Way and the Right Way

Wrong: Avoid behavioral systems using the "when you, then I" method. As in, "When you don't sit still in church, then I feel sad." Any child who struggles to keep up does not need the additional burden and guilt of "I messages."

Right: If your child struggles and is proud when he accomplishes a task, have an "I Can Do It!" jar or box. Whenever he succeeds in something new, you can write that on a paper and he can put it in his jar. Periodically you can sit at the kitchen table, empty the jar, and read all the things he has accomplished. An affirming audience is always welcome at this event as you celebrate the many new things he has mastered.

Or you can create an "I Can Do It!" center: a bulletin board that is to a young child eternal evidence of success. When your child accomplishes something new, celebrate it, write or draw it, and post it. Post that he wrote the first three letters of his name, and post over it when he writes the next letter. What an obvious (literally) achievement record that can be.

Okay, psychology is great, but you must have success to celebrate. Here's where you need to be informed. You need to know what are reasonable expectations, what are the norms, and what are your child's variations.

There are many books detailing developmental milestones, listed by age, for children. Often these accomplishments are divided in these categories: cognitive, communicative, social, and motor skills. For example, cognitive and communication skills expected of a three-year-old might be listed as:

- Puts together a puzzle with five pieces
- Puts two halves together to form a simple picture
- Stacks blocks by size order
- Has a vocabulary of 400—800—1200 words (who's counting???)
- Uses –s on nouns to indicate plurals
- Uses –ed on verbs to indicate past tense
- Uses prepositions
- Matches geometric forms

This book will not reproduce all those lists. But if you have questions or doubts about how your child's development measures up, you may want to explore these topics in detail. There is a definite downside of isolating individual skills and driving yourself crazy. And not all elaborate lists agree. Oh well … see the big picture. If your general knowledge is on target, and if you have good instincts about your child, then you can learn how to help him improve and soar.

Creative Reading Methods

Most children love if you read to them. Seek books that have adventure without too many words. It may help if you read him a short book, all the way through without interruption but with great animation. Then go back to the beginning. Before reading page one again, tell him what to expect: "The pirate is getting on the boat." Then reread that page. If your child likes extensive review, ask him at the end of that page what the pirate did. When you're ready for page two, begin by anticipating: "Now we'll find out how the pirate lost his parrot." Reread page two and then ask your child what happened. Help him focus. Help him put things into words.

If your child has difficulty focusing and/or listening, you need to become an actor and a stage hand. Get his attention by using animation, gestures, voice changes, props. Instead of speaking always in a normal tone of voice, whisper or sing a sentence unexpectedly. Chant, and have him chant a line with you. Dim the lights and use a flashlight; a penlight can focus on the individual pictures or words. Clap or drum together as you repeat theme lines: "The pirate said, 'Where's my sup-per?'" Here's your chance to be both actor and director. How many Hollywood stars yearn for that opportunity—and here it is right in your family room. *Blooming Alert!*

You may want to ask your child to play this game: "I'm going to change something. Listen carefully and see if you can tell me what it is." Then instead of the pirate saying, "Where's my sup-per?" have him say, "Where's my break-fast?" Your child may laugh at those changes and want to make changes himself. Even if his changes don't make any sense, tell him he too can write a story. Take this activity as far as he is interested. Indeed, maybe he can write a story of his own. If so, write it down and promote it. *Blooming Alert!*

There are wordless books—not just picture books with objects, but books with pictures lending themselves to a simple plot. You can explore with your child what he thinks might be happening. If you have difficulty finding such books, you can substitute sequencing game cards, as in (1) a picture of snow, (2) a picture of the sun shining, and (3) the melted snow. Sequencing is a great concept to master, but it isn't quite as exciting as a plot, especially one that ends the way your child decides. If you have oodles of time, you can copy pictures of an action/plot book and cut off the words so your child can create his own plot and details.

Academics Made Easy

For academic areas, be sure your work with him does not reach frustration levels. Too much too soon can cause more harm than good. Be there for him and with him—and enjoy.

Small Motor

If his small motor functions do not measure up to the norms in Chapter 10, you can help. There are so many things children can do that are fun.

Ask your child to cut out newspaper coupons that you will take to the store. This is especially exciting if the coupon is for something he likes. This cutting involves only straight lines, and it doesn't matter if he spoils it. If he frets because the mangled coupon was for his favorite cereal, tape it together on the back and let him start again. Children before the age of six have what child development experts term "functional ambidexterity." That means your child may cut with his right hand for a while, and then shift to his left hand. Be sure you provide scissors designed to cut with either hand. It makes all the difference.

Your child may also like to cut out comics and glue them on a paper. Glue sticks are neat (both meanings) and aid eye-hand coordination. Squeeze-out glue builds hand strength; it's wise to instruct him to use just a little drop on the back. If you're really a glutton for punishment or if you're entering a contest for "Parent of the Year," give him colored or glittered glue to squeeze into letters and shapes and other creative drawings.

If he loves using colored or glitter glue, he may be eager to squeeze it along letters, numbers, or shapes you've lightly written on a paper. And for a real surprise, write his name on a piece of white paper with a white crayon. Give him watercolors to paint on the page. Because white crayon hardly shows on paper, he'll be amazed as his name is revealed. Use it with shapes, numbers, letters, etc., anything he would be excited to discover. He won't even realize he's learning. Once he understands the magic, he will enjoy making surprises on the page for you.

Get your child some small toy cars (cheap) to

drive and park in parking spaces or garages drawn on paper. He can spread yarn for tracks or roads. Use paint samples to match the car color with the parking space color.

Let your child play with playdough. It's great for developing small hand and wrist muscles, and it's a totally no pressure (unavoidable pun) situation for your child. Have him use the playdough on a cookie sheet or some other pan that will confine his materials.

Using that same pan, squirt some aerosol shaving cream or whipped cream for him to swirl and draw and write. Please: instructions and close supervision are vital to differentiate edible from non-edible here. You can add a drop of food coloring for a new adventure, or a drop of two different colors for mixing. What color do red and yellow make when mixed together? Pudding on a pan for finger play is wonderful. Caution: if you are going to videotape your child licking pudding off his fingers, do not use chocolate—use vanilla. Viewers will appreciate your discretion.

Sit with your child at the table with paper and washable markers. Markers have a more dramatic effect than pencils. A game "I Can Do This, I Can Do That," can be used well with this exercise. You draw something, such as a circle. You say, "I can do this," and ask him to draw the same thing. He can say, "I can do that," and draw his circle. Then you put a line through the circle, and ask him to do the same thing with his—with the "I can do this, I can do that" dialogue. Then give him a turn being first, and you copy his doodling. Unlike letters and numbers, there is no right and wrong here. But there is learning.

Have your child help you fold laundry, making his item look like yours. Do it together.

Get discarded keys from a store that makes keys. Draw around various keys on a plain paper, or photocopy them as a group, and have your child match the keys in place.

Arrange buttons, coins, markers, anything in a special order and ask your child to arrange his to match yours. At least to begin, leave your arrangement in place while he matches. Move your items around again and have him match yours. For variation, let him go first. If all goes well, you may try laying out no more than two or three items, then taking them away and seeing if he can remember and reproduce your pattern. This can be as simple or as complex as he can manage.

Use paper clips or snap clothespins to fasten things. Use tongs or tweezers to pick up items. Have a treasure hunt finding coins in sand, wrapped candy in rice, or anything that interests your child while he develops small motor skills. If you're a closet paleontologist, hide dried chicken bones in sand for a historic dig.

You get the idea. Now run with it.

General Factual Knowledge

General factual knowledge is absorbed by children every time we talk with them. So talk with your child. This is to be discussion, not a test. Discuss such things as:

- How many legs does a bird, cow, person, dish, etc. have?

- What color is bread, toast, milk, a balloon, our car, leaves, etc.?

- Which is larger: a car or a house; tree, bush; elephant, lion; etc.?

- What are plates, cars, tables, chairs, clothes, shoes, etc. made out of?

- What do we use water, shoes, furnace, light switch, refrigerator for?

- How does water become an ice cube, day-time become night?

Help your child know about the world. It will inspire him to think about things with an inquiring mind and it can help him master his universe. Help him open doors of his mind.

Cause and Effect

Having a good sense about causes and effects is vital to a child's wise functioning. There is not always a right or wrong answer, but do not let your child's dialogue drift too far astray. Discuss with your child such things as:

What would happen if there were no doors in our house, our car had no gas, Daddy had to sleep in a baby crib…?

Why can't a dog drink out of a cup, we go swimming outdoors when it's snowing, we lift a cow, we see with our eyes closed, a fish use a computer…?

Why do we turn the lights on at night, use a furnace in the winter, use an umbrella when it rains, cook our food…?

Concrete to Abstract Thinking

As children's thought processes mature, they can go from concrete to abstract. Conceptual thinking takes your child from his own concrete, hands-on experiences to the wider world. Whenever necessary or helpful, you may want to incorporate multiple learning aids.*

Play category word games: How are things alike (*you can lay out, as well as say*) mittens, hat, sweater; knife, fork, spoon; then branch out to napkin, plate, fork. (*You probably won't have these readily available, so never mind the multi-aid stuff here*) pig, cow, horse; car, truck, bicycle. Begin with no more than three items and make them familiar entities. You could even start with three physical items lying together on the table and then move to words only. Discuss with your child how and why they are alike. If he can master three items, you could try four. But don't push it too far. He can get the drift at three.

Discuss categories of things and decide which

one does not belong (cow, dog, airplane; *apple, banana, shoe; etc.). Use only three items and make the unlike item obvious, at least in the beginning.

Discuss relationships: a circle and a plate, the right and left hands and thumbs, etc. You can draw around his right hand, then turn the paper over and hold it up to a window; when the light shines through, the right hand now matches his left hand.

Discuss inherent relationships (these big words are for you, not for your child): little, big; up, down; hot, cold. It will be fun if you can use multi-aids: use a little spoon and a big spoon, etc. Exaggerated differences make a stronger impression on children.

With the small motor, general factual knowledge, cause and effect, and conceptual thinking, make the learning fun. If it's a burden for your child, stop or use a different approach.

Auditory Skills

Auditory skills can be improved with practice. Begin by giving your child a simple direction such as, "Touch your nose," or "Open the drawer." Continue by adding a second direction such as, "Clap your hands and turn on the light." Continue as long as your child can follow or is willing to play the game. Let him give instructions to you too, and decide if you have done things in the proper order.

If your child seems not to be listening (which is different from not obeying), try kneeling to his level, holding eye contact, saying his name, even putting your hand on his shoulder. For practice at listening, set a ticking timer and hide it somewhere for your child to find—before the timer goes off.

Play "Twins or Not." Say a word twice, such as "run" and then "run" again. Tell your child they are like twins, just the same. Then say another twins word. Next say two different words, such as "run" and "jump." They are not twins, not exactly the same.

Delayed learners often benefit from more concrete rather than conceptual experiences. To help your child understand the concept of location, you can play, "Your Wish is My Command." Take an item such as a small ball or toy into a room with various furniture pieces. You and your child take turns deciding where to put the item. For example, you may say, "Put the ball/truck/whatever *under* the table." Your child says, "Your wish is my command," and does it. Then he tells you where to put the ball: on *top* of the table, for example. To which you reply, "Your wish is my command," and do it. *Blooming Alert!*

You can have a secret sentence that you tell your child in the morning—something like, "I'll play Chutes and Ladders with you tonight." Whatever the sentence, ask your child to repeat it to you several times during the day. Vary the content and performance times according to your child's ability to succeed.

Visual Functioning

Visual functions include games such as "I Spy," which can safely be played by putting several items on the table (or floor, or bed, etc.). Some things such as colored objects, where you say, "I spy something blue," and your child finds it. Or something round amid various shaped items. If that goes well, expand to spy something in the room. In other words, look for things to look for.

A variation of this can be played indoors or out, but certain factors must be met. The items you use must be identical, such as pink plastic eggs, a matched set of coasters, or yellow pencils of the same size. Start with four identical items, such as coasters.

While your child is out of the room, (can you really expect him not to peek if he's there?) hide the four coasters. Put them in a variety of spots—low and high, although not too high for your child to see. Make the spots fairly obvious to begin, such as on top of a sofa pillow, on the floor under the coffee table, resting against the television set, on the back of the overstuffed chair. Call your child back into the room; see if he can find all four items. As your child's visual functioning increases, use more items hidden in places increasingly more difficult to spot. Hiding them under things (under the rug, etc.) can be great fun too, but that develops a skill apart from visual functioning. *Blooming Alert!*

When it is your child's turn to hide the coasters, he likely will use many of the same places you used. This reflects a preschool developmental stage of perseveration (educational-eze meaning he likes to do the same thing over and over). In this instance, be glad. It lets you find the coasters easily. When your child gets older, he'll hide things in places where you can't find them for weeks—until the half-eaten cheese sandwich under his bed starts smelling … really bad. But for now, it's easy.

Young children love hiding things. A variation of this game uses more items to hide; how large or small the item, how obvious or obscure, depends on your child's interest and ability. If you value the items, always count in advance the number to be hidden. Because … oh, you know.

Visual games can be especially helpful while you are waiting, or doing nothing at all. In a doctor's office, you can play "I Spy." Riding in a car, you can look for colors of cars, count cars or trees, look for letters on signs, or places that serve food, etc.

There are many commercial manipulative games than can help visual functioning, especially matching games. Computers, of course, are predominately based on visual functioning. The right games, used with some moderation, can be a boon to your child. *Double Blooming Alert!*

Eye-Hand Coordination

Eye-hand coordination activities can be great amusement for children, while developing those skills. (We have already mentioned computer games and given you the double blooming alert.) Your child will probably love pouring opportunities—in the bathtub, outdoors, in the sink. Give him lots of containers, funnels, cooking basters, pumps, etc. and proper materials to pour. He may also be enthusiastic about mixing things: instant mashed potatoes with water, for example.

He can drop things into containers: clothespins or pencils in a box, large or small, from varying heights, depending on his ability. Coins in a cup, M&Ms in a bottle, lentils in a pill box.

When it's warm outdoors, let him use big and small paint brushes to dip in water and write or draw all over the sidewalk or the driveway, or perhaps even "paint" the fence or the garage or the house (start in the back). He can do the same indoors with smaller brushes and a chalkboard. You can play a game of having to name the letter or number or shape you or he made before the water evaporates. Commercial paint-with-water books help a child confine his work and have fun at the same time.

Etch-a-sketch games can be good developmental tools, but too frequently children lose interest. Simple dot-to-dot books may amuse, but they may fall in the same category of disinterest. You can have your own dot-to-dot with your child, one that he will probably enjoy because you are together and it is live action. On paper, put a dot. He puts another dot somewhere, and you must draw a line (straight or curvy, your choice) to his dot. Then you make a dot somewhere on the page, and he connects in any way, any color, any available media he chooses. *Blooming Alert!*

Social Functioning

If social functioning is not comfortable for your child, you can be a great help. First, of course, you allow him to operate within the framework of his own personality. He may always be shy. Okay. But shy and awkward and bullish are not synonyms. You can model and role play—your own mini-charm school. First decide what area/s of social functioning you want to improve. Then you can form a plan.

If your child does not talk easily with other children, don't panic. Many don't. Communication and interaction can be a learned skill. Prepare for the great communicator once he starts.

Some children do not know how to enter ongoing play; they stand back and only observe, they take toys other children are using, or they destroy others' work. If your child fits that description, give him the words to say, "Can I play with you?" (Or if you are a true linguist, "May I play with you?" Unfortunately for language purists, that sounds stilted.) Role play how he can interact with other children. Create a friendly environment with other children (in your own home, with one kind playmate, playdates with people who care about your child). Do not let your child perfect bullying habits to get his way with other children. It can be very successful at the time, but long term he'll pay a dear price for that behavior.

Special Circumstances

Of course there are more serious cases with long names and short acronyms: SAD, ADD, ODD, ADHD, PDD, PDD-NOS, autism, Asperger's, etc. On any given day, you may be justified if you find one or more of these describing your child's activity. But if you have serious, ongoing concerns, seek professional help ASAP. Yes, you can do miracles, but you don't have to do them alone.

A high level of activity in your child may be managed better if you do certain things to help calm him. Using these methods does not require a diagnosis of hyperactivity to be effective. If your child is highly active:

- Accept him for who he is. Try not to compare him to others. Do not construct your handling of him according to the casual advice of friends and neighbors.

- Set achievable goals and break tasks down to manageable segments.

- Offer constructive outlets for his energy, including lots of outdoor and big muscle play.

- Don't roughhouse, tickle, or permit sustained wild play with other children.

- Be consistent but firm in discipline and concentrate on a few significant rules. Avoid physical punishment; the idea is to teach that aggression is not acceptable.

- Do not let your child become overtired.

- Try waterplay (indoors and outdoors), playing in a bathtub, with the door open for constant supervision.

- Avoid formal occasions—movies, theaters, and dinners at fancy restaurants—where his fidgeting will enrage others.

- Use Plan BB frequently.

- Do not expect him to nap, take rests, or fall asleep tranquilly at 7:30 as the neighbors' children do. If you let this issue become a battleground, you will all lose; he can stay awake longer than you can. A backrub and/or quiet gentle talks at bedtime can soothe.

- Avoid unnecessary stimulation: loud noises, bright colors, many choices, banging music, mobiles, big rooms with a variety of activities going on at one time.

- Avoid violent, scary, fast-paced, or excessively noisy TV shows, video games, computer games. Hyperactive children are already overstimulated.

- Take time for yourself!

Most children seem hyper at times. Use any of the calming methods listed above ... whatever works.

As you look for new ideas, new ways to teach your child, *your* creative side will blossom. You will probably love it.

Just guess who's blooming now—look in the mirror.

IS THAT ALL THERE IS

Oh, no. It's much more complicated than that.

Child rearing does not have a cookbook precision—put in two hugs and three games and get a sweetie. And just when you think you have figured out all the answers, your child brings up new questions. Drat! (Drat...a nearly naughty oath from the past...but not so long past as to be archaic. If you use #&$!@% words for every minor inconvenience, you have nothing dramatic in reserve for major issues. Besides, all the really naughty-nasty words have lost their shock value from overuse. To get someone's attention, try saying drat instead. If drat is not theatrical enough to turn heads, try the once-almost-scandalous pish-tosh...or think up something else that suits you better.)

It is well known and often believed that children are born with their personalities. This is especially believed by parents who are having the hardest time making things work. You, who have a nearly-perfect child, can credit both nature and nurture—because they are both from you.

In actuality, children do seem to have one of three personality types:

- Easy
- Difficult
- Slow-to-warm-up

The easy child is just easy. It doesn't mean you love him more, but it's easier. As a baby, the easy child sleeps well, doesn't fuss, eats well. As a toddler, he isn't dangerously daring. As a two-year-old, he isn't maddeningly oppositional. As a three-year-old, he loves playing with other children. At four, he doesn't wreck hearth and home. Almost every life experience is an opportunity to enjoy. He smiles a lot, laughs frequently, does what he's asked, conforms readily, completes tasks, adjusts without trauma— he's just easy, which makes everybody's life easier. And he gives you bragging rights, such a "good" child. Thus you may believe and profess that you have done everything right. Okaaaaay. Enjoy.

The difficult child is just difficult. It doesn't mean you love him less, but it's more difficult (for you and for him). Things are too hot or too cold, too loose or too tight, too loud, too bright, too hard, etc., etc., etc.—and they probably are for him. He may have heightened sensitivities. As a baby, he may awaken every time the furnace or AC clicks on. As a toddler, he may be overwhelmed with a new person at the table. As a two-year-old, he may be confused at interaction with other people. As a three-year-old, he may have difficulty with social conformity. At four, he may be a frustrated perfectionist. Often, but certainly not always, this pattern is presented in a bright child. At least it is intensified with a bright child. The difficult child can be so interesting, so clever, and so challenging. The difficult child widens a parent's awareness of everything in the world.

The slow-to-warm-up child is cautious, and then blooms when he feels comfortable. He doesn't jump off the cliff, at least not until he becomes expert in rappelling. He may not talk to strangers, but when he's ready he may enrapture an audience. He may not be willing to try mushrooms before he's fourteen, but may become a food connoisseur once he does. (On the other hand, he may never eat another mushroom in his life—no guarantees.) As a baby, he may sleep only in his bed. As a toddler, he may not taste and test everything. As a two-year-old, he may say "no" even beyond normal oppositional tendencies. As a three-year-old, he may interact only with children he knows well and never speak to strangers. At four, he may pull back instead of charging forward. Only those who know him best, like you, get a glimpse of his true glory. The world will have to wait. And he is definitely bloomable.

Naturally children don't have to fulfill every characteristic of a category. But they do generally approach life within one of these three operational syndromes. You can serve your child best by recognizing which of these three temperaments encompasses him.

Children also seem to have their own inborn level of activity. It seems pre-set if your child needs twelve hours of sleep, or almost none (as it seems to exhausted parents). It's a wondrous fit when parents and children have the same internal system here.

A good fit is helpful in other areas too. If you and your child are both neat and tidy freaks, your home will be an easier place than if you are a neatnik and he is biologically incapable of envisioning order. Sometimes, however, opposites can be a boon. An uptight parent can be soothed by a carefree child, or vice versa.

The most conscientious parent, the best informed parent, the best intentioned parent, must work with the *what is*. It's not possible to learn all the rules, the norms, the developmental expectations and be done with your learning forever, with your PhD allowing you to coast. Every day is a new adventure, a new opportunity to make wise and loving decisions, or not. Remind yourself that nobody, not even you, wins them all. Whenever you feel overwhelmed, remind yourself of the KISS rule: Keep it simple, Stupid.

There are so many influencing elements: health, money, family relationships, jobs. When your baby was first laid in your arms, remember the overwhelming joy, and the dreams? You were ready to conquer the world for your child. Those feelings can glide over you again, every day ... well, almost every day ... well, at least some small part of almost every day—even when harsh realities bump up against them. All families must work within the framework of *what is*. It is not a perfect world, but it is the only world in which we now live. And aren't we lucky!

There are three components to be considered:

Determinism—the body of traits that are just plain predetermined, they come with the child, and they are pretty well entrenched before you ever have a vote. You have little impact here once your child is born.

Behaviorism—how a child learns to function or act. You have a huge influence here.

Perception—how you, your child, and the world perceive that behavior. You can master and triumph here.

It's harsh to say to yourself, "Just deal with it." But you can benefit from the very same words of advice often given to children:

You get what you get,
But you don't get upset.

For those of you who have a different regional accent, you may prefer to use:

You get what you get,
And you don't throw a fit.

When reality sets in, you must acknowledge you are not the sole architect of your precious baby. But you are the prime mover.

TELL ME ABOUT HANSEL AND THE POP-UP TOASTER

As your child develops, his own personality begins to emerge. With great good fortune, he will exhibit all your strengths and none of your weaknesses. In all probability, he'll have some of both—and won't it be exciting to see how it all plays out.

Whatever happens, a good sense of humor is a tremendous asset for your child, for your family, and for you. There can be a drastic turning point in a child's life, but most negative events are just tiny bumps in a very long road. How jarring those bumps are felt will depend on you.

From our file of *True and Almost True Stories*, here are two tales.

The Story of Hansel

In preschool, we had a little boy who was very bright. He knew math concepts far beyond his young age. He could spot patterns before other students, and often before his teachers. We thought him to be a genius…but…

When it was time to go home at the end of class, he/we put all his papers in his school bag. Teachers made certain he had his mittens, his scarf, his hat, his painting, the little car he brought (unauthorized) for "Show and Tell." He lined up with other students and walked toward the pick-up door. From the classroom to the door, all along the path to his mother, he dropped things. He dropped his painting, he dropped his mittens, he dropped his little car, he dropped his scarf, his hat. If he'd had anything else, odds are he would have dropped that too.

The Moral of the Story: Teachers and parents could have been distraught. What a sluggard, what a mess! Instead we smiled, recognizing the wonderful private world of this dear boy. We gathered his things and gave them to his mother, who said thanks so much and nodded knowingly. Didn't Einstein forget to wear socks or something?

Have You Heard the One About the Pop-Up Toaster?

A very interesting little girl came to our school. Her backpack was stuffed with her favorite toys, pictures she had drawn, a cherished note from her grandmother, a comb, scrunchies for her ponytail, letters she had written to tell the world she loved them, and a half-smashed Oreo, contraband of all sorts. We were delighted with her delight...but...

At departure time, we always re-stuffed her backpack. Two teachers would hold the sides together while a third zipped the bag closed.

Every step toward the door, the zipper would nudge a bit...just enough to let a little something escape from the backpack. Eventually her stash would overpower the zipper and erupt.

The Moral of the Story: Teachers and parents could have been distraught. What a sluggard, what a mess (sound familiar?) Instead we smiled, recognizing the wonder of this little girl's world, and what a lesson she could be for us all. She was in love with the whole world—a lesson perhaps to be lost with age and responsibilities, but we hope not.

No one would recommend parental naiveté to the point of child neglect. Yet you can allow your child to dwell in Toyland, even entering it yourself for a time.

- Sing with your child.
- Laugh with your child.
- Dance with your child.
- Joke with your child.
- Play with your child.
- Rejoice with your child.
- You'll all be so glad that you did!

Summary

You want your child to flourish in his world. For you to help him function well, you need to know developmental norms: what's happenin' in the big world around him, and where he fits in.

There are many different kinds of smarts. The focus here is on academic intelligence. The exercises are designed to help you evaluate your child's functioning in various areas: auditory, visual, small motor, large motor, and language skills.

If your child is high functioning, you can expand

his intelligence and have fun doing it. Suggested games and activities can start your creative juices flowing.

If your child is a late bloomer, or needs a little help, here's how you can make him blossom—and even do a little blooming yourself.

It's never boring. Every day is a new adventure. Some things you can control, and some things you can't. The key is knowing which is which.

Attitude is (almost) everything.

Here's the latest, most practical, information on early childhood functioning. Armed with this information, there's no stopping you!

SECTION IV.

CHILD CARE AND PRESCHOOL

HERE'S THE INSIDE STORY

PREVIEW

Your child will be going out into the world...but where, and when, and in whose care? This section gives you "The Inside Story."

Before you hand over your child to someone else, to someplace else, you will benefit from knowing all the options. This section details the various options with the advantages and disadvantages of each.

Classroom developmental lists tell you what your child should be learning and doing.

- Infants
- Toddlers
- Two-Year-Olds
- Three-Year-Old
- Four-Year-Olds

All child care needs are not the same. There is a difference between occasional care, daycare, and preschool—and there should be. You'll find out what and why.

You'll be given information on how to choose the right placement for your child.

Early childhood specialists and educators recommend specific inclusions for the best overall development. The classroom areas list tells you exactly what your child needs in his environment for optimal growth.

When you make the right choices for your child, you *Give Your Child an Advantage.*

GIVE ME THE REAL SCOOP ON CHILD CARE AND PRESCHOOL

At some point, your young child will "leave your nest." You decide where and when. And there are so very many choices. Let's define a few:

- Grandma, a neighbor, a friend
- A caregiver in your home with you there also
- A nanny in your home
- A caregiver in her own home
- Preschool
- Daycare center
- Adoption (oh, no, we've gone too far here)

It must be the best of all worlds to find a caregiver who will adore your child, have all the knowledge and wisdom necessary for expert childrearing, and be available (and free is even better) whenever you call, for as long as you need. If you have that perfect situation, you can skip to the next chapter. Few do.

Basically there are four kinds of care needed:

Sporadic, occasional care
Part-time
Full-time
Extended hours

Each has plusses and minuses.

Relative, Neighbor, Friend

Either sporadic or regular care needs can be met in this way, in your home or theirs.

- \+ This can be the most intimate, loving, comfortable setting for you and your child.

- \+ This can be inexpensive or free.

- \- If it doesn't work out well, it's difficult to "fix."

- \- This may not give your child maximum opportunity for learning experiences or playing with other children.

- \- This may give no supervision of the supervisor.

- \- The caregiver may have her own children who take priority.

- \- This probably has a built-in time limit.

- \- The care depends on one person only.

In Your Own Home, with You There

The next branching out option may have someone in your own home, watching your child there while you work, do errands, whatever, but primarily you would be in the house.

- \+ You can oversee most of the caregiving.

- \+ Your child is familiar with the setting, has his own favorite toys and food, etc.

- \+ If your child is ill or has special needs, you're there.

- You may have to peel him off your leg multiple times a day if he prefers you to the caregiver.

- You may suffer terribly if he prefers the caregiver to you.

- You may need to battle with yourself to stay away from your child.

- Your child may need other opportunities to play with his peers.

A Nanny in Your Home

Should you need regular care, you could have a nanny in your own home.

+ If your child is ill, wants to sleep late, have friends over, the options are easily enacted.

+ The nanny may take your child to lessons, to the library, etc.

+ The nanny may also cook your dinner, clean the house, do all the laundry, walk the dog, wrap the birthday gifts, mow the lawn, grocery shop, give your child piano lessons, and work indefinitely without a salary increase.

- The nanny probably will not.

- The nanny may walk out—quit—without any explanation or advance warning, at any time.

- Who's to supervise the nanny?

In a Caregiver's Home

Some caregivers take children into their own homes, full- or part-time. These may be state licensed and inspected facilities, or not. The need for licensing usually depends on the number of children in the caregiver's home. It's important for you to know about licensing and about insurance liabilities.

+ A home setting may be more intimate, more "homey," than a child care center.

+ There may be fewer children in a home than in a center, perhaps making it a calmer and less regimented atmosphere.

+ There may be more flexible hours for pick-up and drop-off.

+ You may establish almost an extended family relationship.

+ Activities and trips may be tailored to your child's interest.

+ You may be able to send your child even if he isn't feeling well.

- Other parents may send their children even if they aren't feeling well.

- The caregiver might be preoccupied with another child who needs rocking, diapering, refereeing, comforting, having to go to the bathroom, answering the doorbell, talking to another parent, cooking lunch, unclogging the toilet, watching "All My Children" instead of all your children, favoring her own child/ren who rightfully should be #1 with their own parent.

- There may be too many children housed there.

- Who's to know?

- What happens when the caregiver is ill, when her own children are home sick, when she has a telephone call, when she wants to go on vacation?

- If ever the caregiver quits suddenly and unexpectedly, your child's world changes drastically by losing the caregiver, the environment, and all playmates.

Early Learning Center a.k.a. Daycare

A daycare or child care center, often called an early learning center, can be used sporadically, but most often is used regularly for full-time care of children while parents are working. A center should be state licensed and thus routinely inspected by the state department in charge of children's welfare and by health, fire, and safety inspectors. This licensing should also assure criminal background checks and insurance liabilities. Centers vary in the services offered—perhaps infants through grade school— twelve to twenty-four hours a day. Usually they are owned and operated as a private enterprise, a chain, or a franchise. Some are operated as an adjunct to the parent's work place, or to a learning institution's child development program.

+ The center is always there, a familiar place with at least some familiar staff and children.

+ Even though there are changes, the environment generally remains quite stable.

+ Because so many people are on staff, and so many parents are in-and-out all day, there is little opportunity for secrecy of any kind.

+ Usually the only task of a caregiver is to give care to the children—not cook and care, or talk on the phone and care—and if one needs to spend time in the bathroom or concentrate on another child, yet another caregiver is available to give care to your child (mercy, that's how complex it can be).

+ Staff should have ongoing training and supervision.

+ An appropriate developmental program should be in place.

+ There can be stimulating learning opportunities.

+ Children can learn socializing in an environment of equality (as in, no child owns the toys, the mother, the bedroom).

- Centers must have routines to meet the needs of multiple children at the same time.

- Flexibility in scheduling, curriculum, activities, and fees is limited.

- Salaries often are low, classrooms can be under-staffed, and teachers/aides can "burn out."

Appropriate Developmental Programs

For daycare centers, an appropriate developmental program should be defined. Be aware that planned programs and enacted programs may be worlds apart. The following classroom developmental standards are a guide. As you consult them, keep in mind that children develop at different rates, and few children follow every expectation at the exact designated time. The real scoop here is not the book learnin' stuff, but advice gleaned from what really happens when children are together. Some examples:

A baby should be kept in an Infant Room until he can walk. If he moves to the Toddler Room, he'll be crawling while multiple tods are racing around and inadvertently stomping on his fingers. And he'll be hard pressed to get the desired toy before a walking child. He'll have a difficult time reaching things from the floor, and may pull items off shelves that hit him in the face or head. He may be excited about all the new toys in the room, but frustrated that he can't have ready access.

A toddler may want his pacifier throughout the day. But wait—here's what toddlers do. They don't stay in one place long, they get around. A chart of traffic patterns look like this:

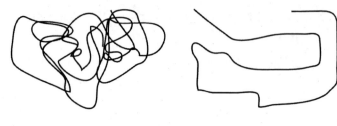

Toddler   *Three-Year-Old*

If you have a toddler in your house, you no doubt have already discovered this for yourself. And while tods are cruising, they put everything in their mouths and they drop everything. Of course a pacifier is a natural lure. (And pinning a child's pacifier to his clothing is no assurance of exclusive ownership... another tod can easily, quickly, readily access that gem.) If a roomful of tods share pacifiers, what germs might be shared? Today is a scary time for really intimate germ sharing. Pacifiers used only at naptime is a safer policy because each child is on his own cot or crib, not sporting a walking taste test for playmates. Even if you are reluctant to limit your child's use of his pacifier, think how you will feel eventually if the center does not have or does not enforce this naptime-only policy. Without this stipulation, think in a few months or years your child may be "off the pacifier," but how much will he yearn if another child is sucking one?

Making adaptations for the spiraling developmental milestones (Listed in the first chapter), a two-year-old may need more creative teacher redirection than a toddler; a four-year-old may need more limiting of overflow language than a three-year-old. Note: Overflow language and overflow motion mean too much talking and moving around, and it's a natural stage for fours as they expand their horizons.

These several explanations, or defense of accuracy, of the classroom developmental lists are added to convince you that this is real scoop, based on vast experience and observation of young children in action. Please believe, as you consult the following lists.

Infant Classroom Developmental Goals (ages 6 weeks to 15 months)

Working on during the 13 ½ months

Eating:	Eating baby food
	Using finger food
	Weaning from the bottle
	Drinking from a sippy cup
Clothing:	Gaining some understanding of clothing
Napping:	Transitioning from morning and afternoon naps to afternoon nap only
Mobility:	Rolling over
	Sitting up
	Crawling
	Taking steps

Ready to move to the Toddler Room

Eating: Feed self some table food
           Weaned from the bottle
           Drink from a sippy cup
           Introduced to a spoon and plate

Toileting: Diapering by adults

Clothing: Must rely on caregiver for dressing

Napping: May want morning rest or quiet time
           Take afternoon nap on cot or crib

Injury: Not able to judge danger or safety

Mobility: Reliably mobile
           Steady in walking

Toddler Classroom Developmental Goals (ages 15 to 24 months)

Entering: see "Ready to move to the Toddler Room"

Working on during the nine months

Eating: Sitting at a low table in a small chair
           Gaining dexterity in using a spoon
           Trying to use a fork/spoon/spork

Toileting: Willing to try toileting in
           coordination with home practices

Clothing: Keeping clothes on appropriately

Napping: Diminishing need for sleep aids
           and pacifiers

Injury:	Beginning to realize cause and effect Not inflicting more than a rare bite, hit, pinch, etc.
Mobility:	Running appropriately and safely
Commun- ication:	Using several words in simple sentences to express wants and needs
Toys and Equipment:	Moving from parallel play to more interactive play Dispelling the toddler belief that any object he sees is his
Circle Time:	Sitting in a group and listening to a short story Joining in rhymes and songs
Cooperation:	Being able to be redirected toward more productive behavior
Verbal:	Imitating sounds Identifying common objects in pictures
Letters and Numbers:	Developing an interest in what they are Developing an interest in rote progression

Shapes and Colors:	Scribbling on paper with crayons
	Playing with playdough
	Painting with brushes

Ready to move to the Two-year-old Room

Eating:	Seat self at a low table in a small chair
	Use a spoon and fork/spork
	Help clean up spills
	Eat without bothering others
Toileting:	Willing to try toileting
	Able to tell if pants are wet or soiled
Clothing:	May assist in dressing and undressing
Napping:	Stay on a cot with adult attention
	Pacifier and sleep aids (blankets, etc.) used at naptime only
Injury:	Begin to develop an awareness of danger or risk
	Show sympathy for others
Mobility:	Walk and run with acceptable purpose
Communication:	Often express basic needs in words

Toys and Equipment:	Begin to interact in sharing of toys
	Put toys away with help
Circle Time:	Reliably stay in his own group in circle or other activities
	Understand and observe physical boundaries
Cooperation:	Begin to make a connection between actions and results
Verbal:	Know a few songs and stories
	Can understand the concept of basic words
Letters and Numbers:	Rote count to five
	Sing the alphabet
Shapes and Colors:	Match one-to-one colors, shapes, and patterns
	Paint and glue appropriately

Two-year-old Classroom Developmental Goals

Entering: see "Ready to move to the Two-year-old Room"

Working on during the year

Eating:	Using a small cup with no lid
	Gaining control of a spoon and fork
Toileting:	Trying toileting in coordination with home practices

Clothing:	Understanding proper use of clothing
Napping:	Staying on a cot without an adult by the side
Injury:	More understanding of cause and effect
Communi-cation:	Using words in simple sentences Using a form of please and thank you
Toys and Equipment:	Moving from parallel play to more interactive play with others
Circle Time:	Phasing out the two-year-old stage of oppositional behavior
Cooperation:	Moving past delight in defiance, such as saying no for the purpose of establishing independence
Verbal:	Increasing vocabulary Expanding realization of the world beyond self
Letters and Numbers:	Understanding that numbers mean something

	Recognizing that letters relate to names and words
Shapes and Colors:	Exploring and enjoying colors, shapes, and patterns Enjoying a variety of media

Ready to move to the Three-year-old Room

Eating:	Sit at a table reliably Use a cup, spoon, fork, and plate successfully Dispose of meal items appropriately
Toileting:	Acknowledge toileting situation, with frequent success in using the bathroom
Clothing:	Assist in dressing and undressing
Napping:	Stay quietly on a cot Pacifier no longer used
Injury:	Begin to develop a conscience
Communication:	Express needs, wants, and likes in simple sentences Use please and thank you
Toys and Equipment:	Realize the fun of playing interactively with others

Circle Time:	More willing to sit for group activities
Cooperation:	Follow one to two simple requests in a row Be willing to learn cooperative play and follow teacher directions
Verbal:	Enjoy conversing Talk of things other than himself
Letters and Numbers:	Realize that numbers quantify things Know the difference between letters and numbers
Shapes and Colors:	Match colors, shapes, and patterns Paint and glue with limited help

Three-year-old Classroom Developmental Goals

Entering: see "Ready to move to the Three-year-old Room"

Working on during the year

Eating:	Serving some food family style Developing basic social skills

Toileting:	Being fairly reliably toilet trained with few surprises Managing most clothing needs
Clothing:	Dressing for the activity or season with reasonable speed Finding and storing his own clothes
Napping:	Staying quietly on a cot without constant reminders
Injury:	Requiring less adult monitoring Understanding that hurting others is wrong
Communication:	Beginning to express social needs in words Telling other children of hurt feelings
Toys and Equipment:	Using toys appropriately and creatively Putting toys away without assistance
Circle Time:	Having fun while listening, watching, and participating Developing a sense of appropriate sharing and participation

Cooperation:	Following three to four simple directions
	Developing a social conscience
	Enjoying cooperative play
Verbal:	Enjoying pretending and extending ideas
Letters and Numbers:	Developing an interest in what letters and numbers can do
Shapes and Colors:	Using paint, glue, and scissors reliably and safely without supervision

Ready to move to the Four-year-old Room

Eating:	Use utensils properly
	Discard mealtime items properly
	Enjoy table socialization
Toileting:	Have few accidents
	Potty by himself, undressing and redressing
Clothing:	Identify his own belongings
Napping:	Identify his own cot, blanket, and sleep aids
Injury:	Report to the teacher any true injury or dangerous situation

Communi-cation:	May tell the teacher of needs or problems with other children Engage in group discussion
Toys and Equipment:	Enjoy cooperative play and share without much discomfort
Circle Time:	Come when called individually Sit at least fifteen minutes without extensive interruption
Cooperation:	Be aware of others' personal space and rights Follow teachers' basic directions Complete simple tasks without teacher prompting
Verbal:	Listen attentively to stories Create scenarios in developmental play
Letters and Numbers:	Understand how letters and numbers may relate to him
Shapes and Colors:	Identify common shapes and colors by pointing

Four-year-old Classroom Developmental Goals

Entering: see "Ready to move to the Four-year-old Room"

Working on during the year

Eating:	Serving family style, pouring his own liquids Cleaning up his own spills Allotting and asking for servings
Toileting:	Learning to anticipate needs and take care of them at the proper time Flushing Washing hands thoroughly and disposing of towels
Clothing:	Anticipating clothing needs
Napping:	Sleeping or resting on cot without disturbing others, with a teacher comforting
Injury:	Differentiating between minor injury and more serious injury requiring adult help
Communi- cation:	Distinguishing between major and minor problems Handling minor problems Verbalizing emotions appropriately

Toys and Equipment:	Sharing or playing alone, being willing to clean up when asked
Circle Time:	Coming when the group is called Sitting twenty minutes Participating when called on Limiting overflow language and overflow motion
Cooperation:	Cooperating with teachers and other children
Verbal:	Engaging in group discussion Understanding nuances
Letters and Numbers:	Rote counting one through twenty Reciting alphabet Recognizing his own written name
Shapes and Colors:	Being able to name common shapes and colors

Exiting the Four-year-old Room—Going "out into the world"

Eating:	Use good table manners
Toileting:	Reliably anticipate and take care of

all reasonable toileting needs, including privacy

Clothing: Keep his clothing stored in proper place
Dress himself in appropriate attire

Napping: Rest quietly or sleep without active teacher involvement

Injury: React appropriately to severity of injury
Take care of minor injuries

Communi-
cation: Use appropriate reasoning skills and words to handle most situations

Toys and
Equipment: Negotiate and plan group activities
Clean up

Circle Time: Participate on a volunteer basis, taking turns
Listen attentively to others
Transition easily
Participate appropriately

Cooperation: Understand and respect need for fairness
Separate easily
Enjoy group dynamics

Verbal:	Explain feelings, motives, and actions of fictional and real people
Letters and Numbers:	Recognize and write some letters and numbers
Shapes and Colors:	Draw a circle, square, and triangle Name eight colors

Every child care program advertises that it uses a developmentally-appropriate curriculum. Ask to see it, in writing, and then observe to see if it's really used.

Working parents often feel such guilt, not being with their children all day. Stay-at-home parents often feel such guilt, not doing more. Turn this lose-lose into a win-win situation. Children in daycare and children at home can be glorious—either way. It's less about what the outside world does and more about what you do. However much your child is with others, he's going to be most like you. Deal with it and rejoice.

There is a fact/myth that children who have been in daycare are more aggressive than stay-at-home children; there is a fact/myth that children who stay at home are more spoiled or dependent than daycare children. These characteristics are as individual as the family involved. Parents of daycare children can, whether from guilt or exhaustion, be very lax with discipline in the few hours they do have their child with them. What loving parent wants to say no during those precious moments? Or what parent wants to enforce no at the end of a long working day? Stay-at-home parents could hardly be that indulgent all day. Those who are create children who are unhappy when they discover they are not the center of the world. Children can be well adjusted and happy, or maladjusted and unhappy, whether they are in all-day care centers or home alone with a parent. For the most part, it's up to you. Either way, stuff the guilt.

Daycare and preschool programs should have a different pace. For example, children in a center for many hours a day need rest time. Along with ample time for free play and exploration and with space for large motor activities, there must be opportunities for quiet and rest. Daycare naptime often is about two hours long. Your child's natural sleep patterns should be considered in choosing a daycare center. Some children (and adults) sleep readily; others have eyes that simply will not stay closed and minds that just cannot be turned off. No child should be made to feel bad simply because he cannot sleep on someone else's schedule. A truly restless child has enough burden without being guilty at naptime. Some centers are more comforting to non-sleeping children.

Enrolling in a good daycare program used by many of your co-workers can be good news/bad news. It's great to have a center that is recommended by a number of people you know and trust. You will have many things in common. The downside occurs if any misbehavior or competition is observed or perceived between the workers' children. How would you feel if your boss' child bit your child? Or... how would you feel if your child bit your boss's child... repeatedly? It does happen, and it can get dicey.

Monitoring cameras can make parents feel more secure about their children's care. It has many safety assurances, but it can backfire if by chance a snapshot view of the classroom does not show the entire picture. A parent may be furious at seeing his child pushed by another, not realizing that his own child had pushed the other one only a few seconds earlier. If your child's classroom has cameras, and if there is any perceived problem, be sure you or someone has seen the entire picture. Also be sure that classrooms are personally visited by management/directors frequently. Camera views are no substitute for personal, professional observation—to see and be seen.

Preschool is a term used in a variety of ways. Usually it means a part-time program with regularly scheduled classes, such as MWF mornings, 9:00 to 11:30, or TTh afternoons, 12:30 to 3:00. Most often ages enrolled in preschool are 3 to 5, or 2½ to 6. Preschool, as its name implies, usually follows the public school attendance schedule with no summer classes. The purpose of preschool is to give children an opportunity to socialize with other children and to prepare for kindergarten. Therefore the pace can be more structured than daycare. In preschool children learn to take turns, to listen and follow teacher directions. Large motor space is less important when children attend only a few hours. Computer play is not a vehicle for socialization, and therefore should not be a lure away from playing with other children. The curriculum is more condensed than daycare; children should not sustain the same level of activity all day as they do in limited preschool hours. How much time is allocated to free play and how much to teacher-directed activities should match your purpose for your child's attendance.

Preschools can be government operated—park district or school district, for example. Or they may be church run, with or without religious component, with or without connection to primary grades kindergarten and up. Some are cooperatives, using parents' help in the classroom. Frequently they are privately owned and operated, either in a home or in a center. Usually they are licensed, although school districts' licensing can vary, and governmental overrides may not require park district, etc. programs to have state licensing. There are standards other than, or in addition to, state licensing, such as accreditation by NAEYC (the National Association for the Education of Young Children).

Often preschools enroll children in the neighborhood. Thus the children have similar backgrounds and feed into the same elementary school. With this in mind, preschools can tailor their programs to blend with the practices of their local public school. While this is an advantage, it should not be the definitive reason for choosing a site.

Mutant programs abound: drop-off care, daycare preschool, family grouped programs mixing different ages, intergenerational programs, inclusion preschools, early intervention, special needs preschool programs, Headstart, preschools focusing on gymnastics or dance or drama or science or music or art...something for everyone, it seems. What a blessing of options.

Early learning systems offer various approaches to learning. Some of those are Piaget (a constructivism theory), Montessori (a maturational system), the Reggio Emilia approach, and a behaviorist approach. Most schools have a developmental or behaviorist approach, which uses guidelines for developmental expectations and watches the child to tailor educational activities to his developmental level. Every system encourages and values play. You have the daunting task of researching and choosing the very best educational system for your child—or you can just send him to the place nearest your house.

As you view a school or care center or home, you can take one of a dozen lists of "How to Choose a Good Program for Your Child." While the lists are not identical, many are quite similar, and they can be found everywhere.

Here's what they don't tell you. Visiting a child care center for the purpose of immediate enrollment, or visiting a preschool for the purpose of enrollment next year, calls for a different set of inquiries. Some of the best ways to determine if it's a good place for your child are:

For Immediate Enrollment in a Program

If possible, go by yourself the first time to view the program.

a. Watch how the children interact with each other. If the children are three and older, do they play well with each other? Do children play with a mixture of others instead of with the same ones? Do they use words of entry such as, "Can I play with you?" instead of hanging back or barging in?

b. Observe how the teachers interact with the children. Do they circulate and extend play by commenting such as, "Could you make another road for the houses over here," or "How high do you think the tower can go?" or "Tell me about your picture."

c. Assess the physical layout, the variety and condition of the classroom equipment. See if the areas of interest are properly designated and include the important developmental activities. Check the availability and accessibility of consumables: paint, various kinds of paper, playdough, pencils, glue, crayons, and markers.

d. Watch the play area patterns of the children. Do they find interesting things to do in all areas of the room, or do they cluster in only a few sections?

e. Pay attention to transitions: the times when children must change from one activity to another. Does the teacher have creative ways of getting the children to clean up, to get in line, to ready themselves for eating, to wash hands, to put on clothes for going outdoors? Or do you hear repetitive nagging, coaxing, whining? Are there such frequent transitions that children are discouraged from extended involvement in their chosen activities?

f. Look around the room. Is it clean? Is it too clean? Are all areas of the room available to the children? Is the room decorated with the children's work? Are too many areas of the room reserved for teacher supplies and off-limits materials? Is it really a child's room or is it a decorator-planned, teacher-convenient room? Does the place shout *yes* to child's play?

g. Are the children busy and interested and active and productive and learning?

After you assess these things, then you may want to pull out your other checklists: the teacher-student ratios, the staff turnover, etc.—all important things. But our a-to-g items are real, behind the scenes, hardly-ever-mentioned important functions for early education facilities. Be sure they're there for your child.

When you have observed the classroom, look at older classrooms. Your child may be three now, and the program may seem A-okay, but how about the Four's Classroom? Will you ever have another baby? How's the Infant Room? When your child leaves the Three's Room to enter the Four's Room, will the school have a meeting with you, with at least one of the "giving" room teachers and one of the "receiving" room teachers? Are the materials all the same, room after room, year after year, or will there be new sensory tables and different home living appliances, etc.? Blink your eyes, and your child will be old enough for college.

If you feel, after your inspection, that your child will "fit in" and be well cared for, then take your child. If you go with your child the first visit, you will be most interested in watching your own child, and will be hard pressed to see how the classroom really works. You have a perspective your child does not. Eating snow cones for afternoon snack may be exciting for your child, but it's not a reason to choose a school. Watching a movie he's wanted to see may be fascinating, but it's not a reason to choose a school. Being the center of the teacher's interest because he's a visitor may be flattering, but it's not a reason to choose a school. Naturally you want your child to feel comfortable in the setting, but a final choice must be made for the right reasons, and only you can decide that.

For Enrollment at a Future Time

Use the same guidelines as the previous a-to-g, with this adaptation. While it's best for you to observe without your child, most parents really, really want to take their child to "see if he fits in." Realize that your child probably will not, and should not, fit into the class he will attend next year. The very best plan is for you to go alone first, to determine if you think it's right for him *in the future*. The best schools have opportunities for enrollees to visit the school with their parents one or more times before school actually starts, with some orientation programs designed to make children comfortable (even eager) to go to school. Also be aware that advance registrations at preschools can be very busy times. Envision your child in that classroom next year. Do you want the teacher to be teaching your child, or to be marketing the class to younger visitors? It's most productive if the teacher can teach, and you can ask questions of a director.

Classroom Interest Areas for Ages 3 to 6

Children learn best when there are specific areas for play. Following are listed various interest areas that should always be included for their use. Designated boundaries should divide interest centers—low cabinets, bookshelves, furniture—something to define clearly that activity for that space. Each interest area should attract child's play; the entire room should be abuzz with children playing appropriately. If any areas are consistently unused, the materials need to be reevaluated and changed. All the interest areas are important for overall child development. Teachers should be circulating, observing the children and extending their play.

When you observe a program for children ages 3 to 6, you should see these "interest areas" or centers.

1. Art

Scissors, glue, collage box, papers (assorted sizes and colors), crayons, markers, paint and brushes, fingerpaint and sensory materials, extenders (rollers, stampers, etc.), chalk, easel, aprons *Note: Paper and/or easel surface should always be ready; supplies should be near a table and an easel.*

2. Manipulatives—Table Toys

Cognitive games, puzzles, small motor toys, literacy materials *Note: These should be near a table for tabletop play so children do not have to use the floor space in front of the cabinet. All the parts should be there. Toys should be readily accessible and easy to put back.*

3. Block and Transportation Play

Large and small blocks, extenders (animals, people, cars, airplanes), pictures, maps, paper for blueprints and plans *Note: This requires an expansive area, and teacher/s need to give input and ideas.*

4. Role Play

Theme, prop boxes, and costumes *Note: The theme should be explained and discussed in circle, with props and theme being changed when children tire.*

5. Housekeeping

Appliances, small table and chairs, food, dishes and pans, dress-up clothes, pictures, flowers, cleaning tools, mirror *Note: All equipment and clothes must be easy to use.*

6. Quiet Area

Books, flannel board, magnet board, puzzles, beanbags/pillows or soft seating, literacy materials *Note: This requires an area away from bustling active play. Television and tapes/DVDs can be used sparingly.*

7. Sensory

Table with water, rice, beads, ice, snow, sand; extenders and tools (sponges, water wheel, measuring containers); sensory boards and cards, bags, etc. *Note: This works best in a more isolated area, not in high traffic areas. Materials should be changed often; tables and materials should be swapped with other classrooms. Cleanup supplies should be readily available and explained to children (towels, brush and pan). Rules must be strictly enforced. Sensory materials should be available daily.*

8. Music

CD/DVDs and tapes, pictures, songs and movement, rhythm instruments, extenders (scarves, balls) *Note: These are not necessary to be available to children at all times. It requires adequate room for movement.*

9. Science

Experiments, books, table or shelf and chair, pictures, unit boxes with hands-on materials *Note: Boxes should be changed frequently.*

10. Theme Center

One-topic themed materials (books, pictures) hands-on materials *Note: Topic materials should be changed when children tire.*

11. Large Motor

Climbing equipment, balancing equipment, mats, riding toys, balls, music *Note: An indoor gym and an outdoor fenced area are both desirable.*

Discipline

Ask to see the school's discipline policy in writing and then observe how often it must be put in use. The best programs seldom need "discipline" and when they do discipline it should be educational and not punitive. Children in centers with good staff and the proper equipment usually are too busy to need discipline. *Time Out* is a term whose time has come and almost gone. Often when a young child is sitting out, he's thinking angry thoughts, perhaps even plotting your premature demise. In emotional excess, it's difficult for him to process "I've misbehaved and therefore I'm not going to do that again." *Time In* is a better recourse—not a reward, but an alternative action that can take him away from out-of-bounds behavior. He can sit in a quiet corner and look at a book, for example, until he calms himself for reasonable play. When he is calm, it is a more opportune time for you to talk with him about his misbehavior. Well-informed adults know the necessary developmental stage when a conscience begins to matter.

Communication

Whatever care you choose for your child, you'll want to know about communication. How accessible is the caregiver? What vehicle/s will be used to confer? How will you know that the caregiver adores your child?

Whoever is expanding your child's world—daycare, preschool, nanny, relative, neighbor—be sure you communicate with those adults. You know how important it is when someone pats you on the back for doing a good job? Well, pat your caregiver on the back and say, "Good job. Thanks for taking such loving care of my child." If that is not true, make a quick change of caregivers. Your child deserves the best.

Summary

Every child goes out into the world at some time. Make this experience, his first experience, a good one. Here's the inside scoop on what to look for and how to evaluate.

Child care means a wide variety of things. Different kinds of care have their individual advantages and disadvantages. A variety of programs need to be defined. Many facilities have specific purposes and structures. When you're ready to enroll your child in some program, here's what to look for. Daycare classroom developmental goals are detailed. Preschool age classroom interest areas are described.

In making the right decision for your child, you help him to feel, "Hello, world. Here I come!"

SECTION V.

KINDERGARTEN/SCHOOL

EARLY TRIUMPH

PREVIEW

Here's where you can really make a difference and ensure that your child has "Early Triumph!"

This section tells you how to assess your child's readiness for kindergarten. Wonderful as your area schools may be, they necessarily have an agenda separate from yours. Schools must serve the best needs of all students; your assignment is to make the best decisions for your child. Schools can't tell you... we do.

You can learn how to evaluate your child's physical, social, personal, and academic readiness. Then you can read how to assess these four individual components collectively from the perspective of what's best for your child personally (as different from what's best for all the five-year-olds in your school).

There's also a little warning for you about Day 1. Read really valuable tips on how to prepare for *The Big Day*.

We all know how important communication is. It's especially important at this juncture since your young child is not yet secure or sophisticated enough to know all the nuances. You'll want to know this information about how to communicate with the teacher/s. Because not all teachers are perfect, you may also need this information to help her communicate with you.

How can you help your child in school? There are many ways other than tutoring or doing his homework. Find out in this section.

Note: If your child will attend universal preschool, many of these preparations will apply. However, do not apply curriculum acceleration, which means expecting kindergarten academic achievement before kindergarten attendance. Using the KISS language, don't expect a four-year-old to be a five-year-old.

WHAT'S A GOOD PARENT TO DO

Assume that you have laid the groundwork success-fully—okay, perhaps not perfectly, but you've given your best to mold a super preschooler. And now the time is here, the real debut: kindergarten. You will not be surprised to learn that we are here to help.

The worst pseudo-reasons for sending your child to kindergarten despite your belief that he's not ready include:

- My spouse (my neighbor, my second cousin, or even you yourself) went to kindergarten at the age of four and turned out fine. *Anecdotal and antiquated information. So what if someone survived early entry decades ago? Things are different now.*

- Our neighbor's child (the other preschool peers, my child's best friend, whoever) is going. *It's like marriage ... not who gets there first but who does it best. Your child may lament for a day or two if he doesn't go to kindergarten with the other kids on the block, but he may lament for sixteen years if he's pushed prematurely.*

- If he doesn't go to kindergarten soon, I'm going to lose my mind. *Well, you may have a valid point here. If you fear some men in white coats may carry you away to a very private place, send your child to kindergarten. Sanity for today; you can cope with the aftermath later.*

So what if a child enters kindergarten before he's ready. If he doesn't do well, he can always repeat kindergarten. You judge if it's better to be "held back" the year before entering…or the year after, which must mean that the child wasn't having a very good time for his first nine months of school. Yet the worst is when a child doesn't fail completely, but muddles through at the bottom and gets passed on to the next grade where he has yet another hard nine months. If a school recommends your child repeat a grade, you can make the best of it and it may have a grand outcome. But it's a risk you wisely avoid if you truly doubt his readiness at the outset.

Schools have a somewhat different perspective: some child must be the youngest in his class. From your perspective, it just doesn't have to be your child. Send your young child to kindergarten only if he likes to do the things they will be doing. If you're not sure, visit the kindergarten to form your own evaluation.

An accurate assessment of your child's readiness is where you begin.

Physical Development

Age is an important factor in kindergarten success. Many studies have been made; statistics abound. You can take several college courses on the subject, or just believe this summary: the youngest to enter a kindergarten class are the most likely to have problems. A summer birthday child, for example, is most apt to be diagnosed as having some learning disability or behavior disorder. This is even more common with boys than with girls. (I don't make this stuff up, I just report it.) It's not statistically reasonable to assume that younger children just happen to be the ones with disorders. Rather, children who have not matured are not ready to learn, to sit still, to listen, to try. A child who doesn't do well in kindergarten starts first grade even farther behind. If your child's preschool teacher suggests he's "not ready," listen to the teacher. Find out if your child really likes to do the things they will do in kindergarten.

Does he like sitting still and listening? Does he like printing, reading, following directions, transitioning when the teacher indicates it's time? If he doesn't like it in preschool, there's little reason to believe he'll like kindergarten. Time to mature, time to play, time to explore, time to march to his own drummer before he must conform. He may have towers to build and playdough to form before he's ready to move on. Just think how much he has matured over this past year—and now he would have to compete with children a year older than he?

Do not be concerned that he might be bored if he is "held back" a year. You may be bored sitting through a lecture on nuclear physics, not because you're too bright, but because you may not have the foundation for it. Children do not get bored hearing the same story over and over. How many times has your child asked you to read the same book again and again; has he ever said, "Oh, no. I've already heard that one"? We are bored when we don't understand, when we're not ready for that information. Children especially benefit when they're somewhat familiar with the information.

If your child is small for his age, be sure he has the words to take care of himself. Young children often say things to smaller children such as, "We're going to play house. You be the baby." Be sure your child can say, "I don't want to be the baby; I want to be the daddy." If other children tell him, "No, we already have a daddy," he can reply, "Then we'll both be daddies." After all, we're not making a family tree here. You can role play with your child, exploring various scenarios and dialogues. Make it fun, make it playful, do not make it seem like an emergency plan.

Conversely, if your child is large for kindergarten, there is no guarantee. Children who grow rapidly can have difficulty managing all those body parts. If they may flail or crash into others, teach them the words of, "Excuse me, I didn't mean to bump you." Otherwise they may be misinterpreted as being confrontational. Large children can find ready followers simply because they're bigger. If your child is the largest in kindergarten, be sure he does not fall into the easy pattern of bullying. While that might work well in kindergarten, it is not a track for future success. Leadership skills are a wonderful asset, but you would want him to lead in the right direction, not be the swaggering leader of thugs.

General health is another important characteristic for determining kindergarten readiness. If your child has any health issues that may deter his learning—asthma that will keep him home frequently, ear infections that hamper his hearing, stomach aches that absorb his attention—be sure he has many other factors working in his favor. If he misses a great deal of school, or if he can't concentrate while he's there, learning will be diminished.

Energy levels seem somewhat pre-set. A highly active child may have a difficult time sitting still, waiting his turn, being quiet, finishing the task. A lethargic child may need more time to work, more teacher direction, more stimulation, more reassurance.

The ability to concentrate also seems somewhat biologically or neurologically impacted, if not determined. Some children can find it hard to be forced to transition. Should your child have the wonderful ability to be totally absorbed in something, you may need to work on transitioning. You can give a forewarning, "In two minutes, you'll have to put the (whatever) away and get your coat on." Give him practice at leaving one thing and doing another, before he starts to school where they may not even have advance notice.

Social Development

Such an important component for school happiness and success! Self-confidence can do wonders, and lack of it can be a sad deterrent. Being your child's cheerleader is not sufficient to give him confidence. He must believe that he can do it, and if he can't yet do it, it doesn't much matter; he'll do it soon.

Self-confidence means assurance with peers and teachers. No child should have to hold constant vigil until his teacher gives an approving nod or smile. No child should have to get an okay from peers to free him up to play. Your child should be told early on that he should do what his parents say, he should do what his teachers or caregivers say, but he does not have to do what another child says—period. If your child seems to lack social skills and self-confidence, invite another child to play at your house. Then branch out from there.

As a quirk of fate, sometimes opposites do attract so that a very timid child may be enchanted with the daring of a rascal. He may even tolerate abuse from the rascal, or follow the rascal into troubled waters and into trouble himself. The following child may be sad at being hit, kicked, pushed rather consistently by the rascal, and yet go back again and again. A teacher, like a boxing referee, can order them to separate—but a bell in their heads goes off and they're back at it, by their own choice. At some point a timid child gets more savvy and finds better play options, but it may take quite some time.

Social development requires acceptance of structure. A child who marches only to his own drum may march alone, may risk injury, may miss some really good stuff in this world. In kindergarten, children must all go outside when told; no one can opt to stay alone indoors and play. If your child is still manifesting the two-year-old oppositional functioning, a kindergarten teacher will have little time and less patience to coax, cajole, and motivate him at every turn. When told to line up at the door, that means everybody line up at the door. When told to put away toys or pencils or schoolwork, everybody must put away. When told to stay within bounds on the playground, a child who runs and hides in neighboring bushes can be in serious danger. When told not to climb up the slippery end of the slide, a child who defies can be hit in the face with down-coming feet. Each instruction or transition does not require a high level summit conference—just sit in your seat or get ready to go home—no Geneva Conference will he held here.

Self-control is helpful. Some children speak in a voice too soft even to hear; others use a voice fit to lead an after-touchdown celebration. A moderate voice is a benefit. Using appropriate words instead of tears, pushing, or kicking is a benefit. Emotional responses appropriate for the situation gain great respect for a child. One who shrieks at nothing is hardly credible when he shrieks at something.

A good sense of sharing is truly a blessing. Any

child who has great pains taking turns is not gonna' be happy in a classroom of twenty to thirty children. Taking turns is a double duty, recognizing when he must give up, but also recognizing when it is rightfully his own turn. In kindergarten, it may be easier for your child to share things than to share the teacher's attention. At home with you, if his shoe needs to be tied, you probably just tie it. At school with a teacher who is reading a book to the class, she can hardly stop everything to tie one child's shoe. Be sure your child understands that the teacher is not ignoring him, the time just might not be right. He may not get to talk whenever he wants in group time, but his turn will come. If you think your child may have difficulty here, he may improve with more time in play groups, in preschool, in sporting activities, or in settings such as the library story time where he is one of many.

Personal Development

He is darling, of course, but can he find his coat? Label all loose parts…with a permanent marker. Can he find the bathroom at school, and once there can he meet his toileting needs? Does he know how to tell the teacher he's worried about finding his bus after class, or the little truck he had in his school bag? Can he tell the teacher if there's a big problem with another child? And if the problem is not big, will he know the difference? He must be responsible for his actions and his expressions, and that's a big order for a little kid. If you can give him perspective, he's a fortunate little kid.

Academic Readiness

Your child's preschool teacher is probably the best determiner of this. Remember that we are talking about academic readiness, not intelligence. A very intelligent child may not be ready to do what they do in kindergarten.

All the developmental norms listed in the previous chapter can help you know how to evaluate your own child. Chapters 11 and 12 have many suggestions for expanding his academic development.

Overall Readiness

We all realize the benefit of a successful school experience and a good start in kindergarten. This can, unfortunately, create much pressure to make the right decision about whether a child is "ready," and if so what we can do to maximize that readiness. These guidelines may help.

- Physical Development: Is your child's physical developmental level going to allow him to do the things he needs to do in kindergarten—sit still, listen, follow directions, coordinate eye-hand movements, stay healthy?

- Social Development: Is he ready to go out into a larger group, relatively unprotected, in student-teacher ratios of perhaps one to twenty-five or more?

- Personal Development: Is he ready for the responsibilities of school?

- Academic Readiness: Does he like to do the things they do in kindergarten?

You may have strong goals, admitted or not, for your child's future. If in your heart you really want a football player, don't send your small child to school prematurely. Caution: red shirting in kindergarten must not run afoul of state and local education laws. If you yearn for a genius, don't rush early entrance unless your child is about as eager as you are. You have every right to harbor goals, but be honest with yourself. Some parents say, "I just want an average child." The adverb "just" speaks volumes, because hardly anyone says, "I just want an Einstein." Realize that an average child is wonderful ("A" or "B" is the grade representing an above-average child; "D" or "E" is a grade representing a low-functioning child). By definition, average means "C." Be clear in your own mind what your expectations are. Your child may or may not meet those expectations, but chances are much better if you define them accurately.

If you decide he's ready and he is going to kindergarten, here are some things you need to do.

In the summer, he may sleep late, watch television while he munches cereal bites, get dressed mid-morning...and then the first day of school is here. "Hurry up, eat your breakfast, get dressed, it's time for school, you're going to be late, oh woe is me—and you." Don't let that shock happen in your house. A week or two before school starts, get into a routine that matches his school schedule. Get him up at the same time he'll wake for kindergarten. Eat and dress for school (no dawdling now). Then do a dry run. Take him to his school-to-be; let him play on the playground. Look in the windows of classrooms. If he'll take a school bus, see if you can drive to the bus lot to look around.

If he is a bit reluctant to leave you, be sure he spends time with others away from you before the first day of school. You might even have him ride with a neighbor and a child for a dry run.

Should he have any special food or medical needs, be sure the teacher is aware of this. Don't assume that filling out papers will do the job; if it's important, tell the teacher personally.

Give him the words he may need to say: "I have to go to the bathroom," "Where will my mommy pick me up," "I can't find my jacket," whatever.

Hopefully the school will have had an orientation and the children will be somewhat familiar with the layout, the classroom, and the teacher. Even if your child is an extrovert who goes gladly into the brave new world, you don't want him to be in a room where other children are crying.

Tell your child what you will be doing while he's at kindergarten. Tell him he'll be playing and learning things, and you'll be home washing breakfast dishes, making beds, doing the laundry...or at work in front of the computer. Which is probably the kind of stuff you do anyway. After school when you pick up or wait for the bus arrival of your child...often you all go to McDonald's, ToysRUs, Best Buy, the park. Your child has little way of knowing that you're not having a fabulous day at McDonald's by yourself, without him. And if there are younger siblings in your household, be sure to tell your new kindergartener that the baby will be sleeping, or playing in his crib, or something definitely not involving cooing with you.

And the last instruction is for you: *do not cry*, at least not where your child can see you. Conversely, do not celebrate too openly. Address the situation with moderation...until you are out of his eyesight. What happens then can be another one of your little secrets.

IS KINDERGARTEN READY FOR ME

We can hope that your child has a teacher whose personality is nurturing for him. Most kindergarten teachers are loving, kind, wonderful people—there to help the children learn and thrive. Yet there can be a mismatch of personalities.

Schools seldom allow parents to select their child's classroom teacher. If your child is assigned a teacher whom you know to be "wrong" for your child, you can try for reassignment. You would need to make a convincing, reasonable case to succeed. And your plea must be for the welfare of your child. The fact that you like to sleep late in the morning and thus want your child to be reassigned to afternoon kindergarten, just won't make it. But if your child needs strong guidance to function well, the school might consider changing him from an easy-mark teacher to a sterner taskmaster. Documentation from a preschool with facts supporting your cause may also help.

Whether your child's teacher is first or last on your wish list, make the year the best possible. Most schools and classrooms welcome volunteer help. If that's a possibility for you, it has many advantages. You can become familiar with school policies and personnel, and you can make the class better. You can judge for yourself if your child has any areas of deficiency and learn ways to help him. Volunteering gives you a chance to bond with a teacher as you work together toward better education for all the children. It also allows you to see how dedicated the teachers are, and to tell them so.

A kindergarten teacher usually has twenty to thirty or more children. Some of these children have never been exposed to a group setting before; others have been schooled, either in preschool or daycare, for years. What a disparity for one teacher. If your district has universal preschool for all children, the first year of attendance may be at three years old, or four years old. The principle still holds. The first required attendance year brings a motley group. What an advantage your child can have there.

Be sure your child understands how to get in a line, how to raise his hand if required, how to sit in a circle, how to listen. Less esoteric, but perhaps more important, is toileting. Listening to a good book can be more captivating than heeding a bathroom warning. We buy darling clothes for our children, sometimes little outfits that take three adults to unbutton. Especially if your child "waits till the last minute," send him to school in clothes that are easy to take off...with instructions.

> *One darling little girl, in our school for the first time, went into the bathroom. She stayed for an unusually long time. The teacher checked frequently, "Jennifer, are you all right in there?"*

Answer, "Yes." Then, "Jennifer, do you need help?"
Answer, "No." Eventually Jennifer came out of the
stall ... stripped naked. She had taken off her shoes
and tights, removed her panties, shed her skirt and
shirt, not realizing that all she needed to potty was
pull down her tights and panties.

Unless you're really sure of your child, don't assume he'll know what to do in the bathroom. Particularly at the beginning of the year, play it safe and instruct him as he dresses. If you think your child might have a toileting accident at school, put an extra pair of clothing in his backpack.

In our school, yet another teacher with yet another
child with yet another bathroom delay called to
him on the other side of the door, "Robert, are
you all right in there?" Answer, "Yes." After
many concerned inquiries, she discretely asked,
"Robert, are you having a BM?" After some
pause, the indiscrete answer came booming back,
"Teacher, does that spell POOP?"

So be sure your child has some knowledge of frequently used common bathroom terms.

Other than extra clothing, discourage your child from taking unsolicited items to school. There are plenty of things already at school for children to do. Especially if your child is a pop-up toaster, check his school bag for contraband before sending him off.

And remember Hansel? If your child drops everything, be sure everything has markings he can identify as his own—permanent markings. On outside clothing such as coats and hats, you may not want to have his name too visible. But if he's really a classic Hansel case, you could sew or iron on tape in an orange X, or a purple pompon…something everyone in his room would instantly know belongs to him, even when it's lying abandoned on the playground. By the way, have you ever checked the lost and found at an elementary school? A good winter coat…one boot…*one* boot? Do you suppose the owner hobbled home? Kids can lose anything.

If any areas of your child's performance or functioning require special attention, be sure the teacher knows. Exactly how and when to "share" this information can be tricky. If you have the perception of a seer and the tact of an ambassador, it helps. Oh yes, and the heart of a saint.

Things your child's teacher needs to know immediately are any serious health issues or any irregular school pick-up arrangements. If there is reason to anticipate a crisis of any kind, be sure the teacher has all current numbers where you can be reached. And be there, where you say you can be reached. And be sure your cell phone is turned on, loud ring when necessary or vibration when dictated, and has bars. And answer the phone when it does ring. Don't make the school send the CIA to locate you…don't enroll in the Witness Protection Program. If your number changes, or your place of work changes, or your home address, or your emergency contact person changes, be sure you inform the school immediately. If your child is bleeding and your employer listed on the emergency sheet says you haven't worked there for three months, it's distressing to both the school and to your child.

Teachers need your cooperation in many ways. Fill out and return all required paperwork, on time. Don't make the school come after you for your child's immunization records either. When field trips are scheduled, send your permission slip before the day of the trip. When the teacher asks parents to send stuff, such as an oatmeal carton, send an oatmeal carton, and send it before the deadline date. Check your child's backpack daily to see if there are any messages from school. Your child very likely will not remember to give you the notice saying some students have head lice. Furthermore, it's discouraging to a teacher when she discovers you haven't taken out your child's work for four days. Don't you care what they're doing in class? Don't you care that your child has done wondrous things, or that he needs help with spelling? If you're not interested enough even to look at his work, how interested should the teacher be?

At the beginning of school, find out what vehicle/s you can best use for communicating with your child's teacher. Some morning right before school, your dog may get loose, your child may be sick at his stomach, Grandma may be taken to the hospital—things happen in life—and it may be important for you to tell the teacher before your child gets to school. This is not the time to research how to contact the teacher; plan ahead. Perhaps the teacher has e-mail that she reads every morning before the students come. Perhaps the school office has a recording/voicemail system for individual teachers. Whatever their communication method is, have that information at hand. The teacher should know whether your child is crying because his dog is gone or he's worried about Grandma, and it's best that she not be caught totally unawares if you child vomits in the classroom.

Of less urgency, but still important, is an open discussion of circumstances you observe with your own child. Not on the first day, but in a timely way, tell his teacher if he has a high activity level.

> *Matthew, very highly active Matthew, came to our school. He was bright and interesting, and probably biologically unable to sit still for much longer than 2½ seconds. We were working with him, making some progress, and then it was time for him to go to kindergarten. His preschool teacher suggested that his parents might want to discuss his activity level with the kindergarten teacher at the beginning of the year. His parents were determined they would not, could not, reveal his condition…because he might be "labeled" at the grade school. We did understand their concern, but could they possibly think the kindergarten teacher wouldn't notice if they didn't bring it up?*

Guess what... she noticed.

If your child fits this description, check to see if his seat faces toward the noisy, active block area or toward the quiet reading area. If you know him to be easily distracted, ask the kindergarten teacher to give him a seat facing away from, rather than toward, the action. After all, somebody has to sit in the front and somebody has to sit in the back, somebody has to face the center of the room and somebody else faces the wall, somebody sits next to a rambunctious child and somebody else sits next to an introvert. The teacher will notice on her own if your child is easily distracted, but it may take her until November to do something about it. Well, if you had to handle twenty-five neo-kindergarteners by yourself, wouldn't you appreciate a heads-up?

Or your child may be very particular, expecting near perfection in everything he does. It may even be December before an even great teacher realizes why your child is slow. He's erasing and erasing, he's thinking and planning how to do it just right, he's bolstering his courage to try this new thing... and he may be very quiet about it all. Of course, the teacher needs to deal with the rowdy ones first. Just tell her about your child's high expectations for himself. Otherwise she might mistake him for being "immature" or "underachieving" or "learning disadvantaged." Be certain you yourself do not label your child in front of your child. Never say to a teacher within your child's earshot, "He's shy," or

"He's too hard on himself." Say to the teacher when your child can hear, "He will blossom in your class." Victory for all!

Parent-Teacher Conferences
(and what you can do to make them better)

Scheduled parent-teacher conferences are a wonderful vehicle for communication. They also are very time consuming for a teacher. Her preparation is important, but so is yours. Before the conference, give some thought to what you want to learn from it. If there are specific questions, concerns, or goals that you have, start the conference by telling the teacher of this. If it's a reasonable possibility, write a short note to the teacher in advance to let her know what you may be asking so she can be prepared. Don't let her spend 90% of your allotted time talking about his addition and subtraction skills if you already know he can do log rhythms, but you wonder if he's making any friends. Don't have the teacher heap praise of your child's social skills for fifteen minutes when you know he has three siblings, seven cousins, and twenty-four friends in play group and the interactive skills of an incumbent politician, but has the academic interest of a slug. So begin by telling the teacher if you have areas you need to know about.

There are ways teachers should talk to parents and ways that parents should talk to teachers.

It helps if the teacher knows she can be honest with you. If she brings up any issues, hear them with an open mind. You may not agree, but you may have insight that can be helpful. If you seem hostile to her concerns, she may mask her information, she may soften her message with educational-eze language, or she may even scrap the whole discussion. Whether or not you agree with her conclusions, you need to hear them.

There should be no labeling or name calling of children in a conference: hyperactive, shy, selfish, uncoordinated, immature. And no accusatory generalities: he disturbs the class, he talks too much. College level education classes can teach teachers educational-eze, which can be a mystery to parents. After acing Education 101, a teacher may say to a parent, "He's immature." What does that mean? The teacher should describe for you what your child *does*. Does he fall asleep at his desk, does he drool and spit, does he hit others, does he cry? She needs to tell you what makes him "immature." Is he the last child in the class to read *Clifford, Book* 3, or to add 1 + 1 and get 2? If you know more precisely what your child does, you may be able to help. You can warn your child not to spit. You can teach your child alternatives to crying. You can tutor your child about 1 + 1. But you cannot tell your child, "Don't be so immature." Well, you can tell him, but that won't help.

If the teacher uses any labeling, name-calling, or

generalities in evaluating your child, redirect her by saying:

- Tell me what you see.

  Instead of telling you that your child is immature, she should say that when she sees him playing with other children, he cries. When she watches him do his assigned work, he loses interest quickly and does not finish in time.

  You, the parent, need to have a clear picture in your mind of what your child is *doing*.

- Describe for me what happens.

  Instead of telling you that your child disturbs the class, she should describe when, how, to whom, what time of day, and during what activities.

  You, the parent, need to know the circumstances. If, for example, he kicks the blocks, that can be very different from talking out of turn.

  Instead of telling you that your child talks too much, she should describe when, to whom, for what purpose, and during what activities.

  You, the parent, need to know if your child is talking to ask for help with his work, talking to help other children with their work, interrupting story time to ask a question about the story, or interrupting to talk about a totally unrelated subject.

- What things have you tried, or will you do, to make this better?

  If he talks during circle, has the teacher tried putting

him up front, next to her...or away from the same
child to whom he always talks?

- May I come and watch?
  If you observe a class, it's good to go as a volunteer rather than as a monitor.

  After observing, you need to ask the teacher if the behavior you saw is typical behavior for your child.

- What can I do to help?
  A teacher should be delighted that you want to work in partnership with her.

You can help best with the right information. We realize that teachers should not compare children, but you do need a context in which to put the information she gives you. She may say, "Your child draws a circle and a rectangle." So what does that mean? Is he the only child in the class who can draw a circle and a rectangle? Or can all the other students draw a circle and a rectangle and a trapezoid and a rhombus? When the teacher shows you examples of your child's work, you need to know if it's an accurate sample of his performance.

(and what the teacher can do to
make the conference better)

For young children ages three to eight, their expected academic performance is generally standardized and objective, while reports on their overall performance can be quite subjective.

During the conferences when teachers give their opinions about your child, this is what the best teachers do:

1. They address the goals important to you. They can do this by asking you things such as:
   - How does (your child's name) like school?
   - What would you like (your child's name) to get from school this year?
   - How do you think things are gong for (your child's name) so far?
   - Does (your child's name) talk about his friends at school?

If the teacher does not ask any of these questions at the beginning, you introduce the information. It's important for the teacher to know.

2. They keep an overall view, not putting too much emphasis on individual skills and performance. They realize it is the whole child that is important.

While you want to know the academic details, they should not override your child's person. If his handwriting is poor, it certainly does not make him a failure. If overall performance lags behind others, that's something to work on.

3. They do not tell you about other children in the class or about their own children.

You would not expect a physician to tell you about her own child's appendectomy; you should not expect a teacher to tell you about her own child's math ability or hyperactivity. Just as you would not want the teacher to tell others about your child's problem in class, you should not hear about problems of other children in the class. Information about your child, and other children, should be private and respected. You certainly should not hear stories about other children such as, "Anne doesn't play well with Suzie," and "Johnny hits the other children."

4. They clearly are for your child, telling you when you've done a great job, letting you know they like your child.

5. They state your child's achievements and actions in a positive way.

6. They give answers and possible solutions or courses of action for any problem.

7. They describe behavior, with no labels or name-calling.

8. They tell what happens to your child, not what happens to their class.

9. They remember that they are the professionals and what they say carries great weight. They should not alarm parents without reason.

10. They rejoice with you in the new accomplishments of your child.

The best teachers dialogue in these ways:

1. We are working on…

   - I am going to try (some course of action) to help him.
   - Is this how you see him at home?
   - Is this what you would expect from him at school?
   - He is liked by the other children in his class.
   - I would like to see him be more adaptable.
   - He loves to play with the children and have fun.
   - He is learning to take turns.
   - I'd like to see him move into the next developmental stage of…

2. A timid, obedient child might be encouraged to take more risks.

3. A child who is highly active may need to have his attention span lengthened and the teacher may discuss with you methods to focus his attention.

4. Although an aggressive child may be a very successful adult, he does in the meantime have to be in a classroom throughout his school life. Therefore, it helps if he can adapt somewhat to the structure.

5. We try to give children some opportunity for freedom of choice and creativity and some opportunity for structure and following directions.

Getting to and from School

How your child gets to and from school can have an impact on his education. Some children take a school bus. Usually children love the bus stop; it can be a positive part of socialization. But schools cannot be accountable for what happens at your child's bus stop. If there is a problem, you need to know. If it's an awful problem, feel free to intervene. We realize that every child needs to learn to "stand up for himself," but not at age five. In fact, if a husband waiting for a metro-area bus were attacked by another rider, his wife would not tell him to "go right back out there and hit him back." They would call the police—immediately. How could we expect a kindergartener to defend himself against an older child, or a group of them? You have the right, in fact the parent's responsibility, to protect your child if he is in real danger. If necessary, stand at the bus stop with him until he boards. Once your child is on the bus, the driver does have some responsibility. If your best efforts still do not stop the problem, you may have to drive your child (if possible) or walk with him to the next bus stop. Just don't think you must stand by and take no action. He can learn later the lesson of self-defense on a more level playing field.

Your child may be in a neighborhood carpool. Children can have great fun in a carpool...or not. If, when it is your turn to chauffer, you find the children needling and teasing each other, find ways to redirect misbehavior. Some, but not all, cars are entertainment complexes—bigger than your parents' first house. If you have the equivalent of a Cinemaplex 30 in your vehicle, keep a constant supply of DVDs available, even if you must get new ones from your local library. If you have a car, just an ordinary car, then you'll need to be more creative. You can even do this in a Cinemaplex vehicle. Sing silly songs, play "I'm thinking of..." an animal that has stripes, a number between five and ten, whatever. Look for letters on signs or colors of cars or numbers on license plates. Just stop the madness however you can, and have fun. And if you have reason to suspect another parent's car is a hotbed of mischief, share your methods with her. It may not be your responsibility, but your child is in that car and you want the best for your child on his way to school.

School arrival time can also be important. If your child enjoys unsupervised playground play, it's okay if he's one of the earlier arrivals. If he's apprehensive about this, be sure he doesn't get there too early. You don't want him walking into the classroom already unnerved. Obviously if he's bussed, you have little control over his arrival time.

The opposite circumstance is the child who frequently comes late to class. He has little control over this, but he may suffer when he comes in late—

perhaps missing teacher instructions, or formation of groups, or songs, or even his turn—never really knowing what he has missed. Anyone can "run late" on occasion, but habitual tardiness can bring trauma to your child, whether tardiness is in arrival or pick up. Don't do that to your child.

Be sure that you have good, open communication with your child. You probably have words of wisdom to help him deal with unfortunate situations, but you can only help him if you know what those situations are.

The #1 Rule for any school problem: Do not show alarm. If you're worried, your child will be frantic.

Kindergarten is the beginning of your child's formal education. A good start is a huge advantage for your child, and for you. Make it a success story.

Summary

So it's time for your child to go to kindergarten.

You can assess your child's readiness in developmental areas of: physical, social, personal, academic, and overall.

Children need to cope and learn at the same time.

There are many practical things you can do to help him prepare for a good experience.

This is a new experience for you, too. Prepare yourself.

An informed parent can make a huge difference.

Talking to the teacher and asking the right questions makes the most of parent-teacher communications.

After all the school preparation, your child is there now, and you can still help him adjust.

Early triumph sets the course for the rest of his life. What luck he has you to guide him!

SECTION VI.

THE ADVANTAGE FACTOR

WHAT YOU CAN GIVE YOUR CHILD

PREVIEW

This chapter reveals "What You Can Give Your Child"; it's The Advantage Factor.

You will learn more about the third component that makes up your child's personality: perception. A functioning scale shows you how to interpret his abilities and behaviors, in his favor.

This section articulates how your actions mold your child and how your goals influence both his and your lives.

You will learn methods and approaches to make you a creative problem solver and the benefits of being pro-active.

You will read about setting the pace for living and the necessity of trust.

And you will be reminded of the importance of character and courage.

THE ADVANTAGE FACTOR

The greatest advantage you can give your child—ever…

is…

is…

is

YOU

(As you would suspect, detailed instructions follow.)

Any child who has even one person who loves him madly has a great advantage. If that one person has good sense and accurate information, the child has an even greater advantage. And if a child has more than one person (who loves him madly and has good sense and accurate information), it's the greatest advantage!

But we're starting with the reader: you rearing your child. As discussed earlier, there are three main components to the miracle of our children:

- Determinism—characteristics imprinted before birth

- Behaviorism—behaviors learned through life's experiences

- Perception—how you view life, what you make of it

Let's talk about perception. Some other person could be critical of your child's reluctance to interact, declaring him to be unsociable. You see him as a keen observer, gathering information someday to write *The Great American Novel*.

Another person could be annoyed with your child's talking too much, which you know is a wonderful ability if he someday is to be a mover-and-shaker.

A functioning scale can help you find perspective. This example is for the level of activity of a child:

Hyperkinetic	Hypokinetic

The x in the middle represents average behavior. It is not the goal, but the norm. If your child is totally, unrelentingly hyperactive, he would be charted all the way to the left, which is extreme. (We're not talking neurological diagnosis here; if necessary, consult a professional.) If your child seldom moves, he would be all the way to the right, which is extreme. But assume your child is highly active; you might mark his usual behavior about midway between the center and the left. He could be described in words as "too hyper," which has a negative connotation. You, of course, see him as "having so much energy to do different things, so much enthusiasm for life"—because it's true, and because energy is a good thing. When you love someone, you see the good in what he does. Use the scale to define where your child functions, and to find value in that. If the notation gets too far out of line, do a little tweaking with him.

Use any terms or attributes you want to create your own functioning scale for your child. You may want to start with such traits as:

Dependent	Independent
Quiet	Noisy
Lethargic	Impulsive
Patient	Impatient
Loner	Requires companions
Withdraws	Dominates
Distractibility	Perseveration
Follower	Bossy
Introvert	Extrovert

Unless a trait is quite extreme or detrimental to your child, find the good in it. So your child "requires companions," what a social success that can be. He's "bossy," there's a leader. An "introvert" can be a deep thinker. If you feel that a nudge in a different direction would be progress, go ahead and nudge. The important thing is to see the value in his own personality. What an advantage, having someone love him for what he is. Human dignity and worth begin with loving a person for what he is. It's a great, lifelong lesson from you to your child.

There are probably 10,000 books on how to...*whatever*...for parents and caregivers of young children. No single source or book can answer all your questions. You may read a book of 500 pages and find only two paragraphs applicable to your and your child. Even more frustrating is when you read a dozen diverse books and begin to think every paragraph of every book applies to your child. By the time you've read them all and tried half the recommendations, your child is confused and grown.

The purpose of this book is not to psychoanalyze you or your family, because each family circumstance is unique and fluid. The purpose of this book is not to answer every question, because just when you get an answer the question changes.

The purpose of this book is to jumpstart your own creativity.

No one loves your child more deeply than you do. No one observes your child more keenly than you do. And no one impacts your child more pervasively than you do.

How we care for our children usually mirrors our own parents' parenting style. If you had fabulous parents, pass it on. If not, start your own legacy.

Armed with general information about developmental stages and norms, you can come up with the best plan of action. Only you know what's possible in your situation; only you can and will hold constant vigil to see what works.

Consider honestly your goals for your child. Expecting your child to behave one way when your own values are opposite (or ill defined) can cause angst for you both. For example, envision a trip to the market. Your child is bored and starts rearranging stock on the shelves. Oh no, people are watching. So you say in a voice loud enough for all to hear, "No, Johnny, don't do that." Then you ignore his continuing action, just as Johnny ignores your words. He knows you don't mean it, you know he knows, etc. It's more than a point of being consistent for following through, it's really a clash of your own values. You want any and all spectators to view you as a conscientious parent, yet you don't want Johnny to be thwarted. Or perhaps you simply don't want Johnny to scream.

Mixed messages = anxiety.

Constant mixed messages = chaos.

You can be a creative problem solver. It's contagious and self-perpetuating. Think of one fun solution to a problem situation and two more ideas will pop up. Better yet, think of one fun activity to preclude a problem situation.

As an exercise, think of how many possible ways

you could divert your Johnny when you know he will destroy the shelves at the market:

- Give him a "list" of items you want. It need not be your complete grocery list…it need not necessarily be all words; it could have some pictures (even ones he drew himself, or ones he cut from the market flier). Have him check off each item as it is put in the basket. You be the reader if necessary.

- Play "I Spy" for items. You are able to read the aisle categories, so you change your target to match the inventory. When the cereal aisle comes up, see who can spy Cheerios first. Next aisle is dairy, look for chocolate milk or soy milk.

- Look for items in a wrapper, in a can, in a box (round or square or rectangular).

- Categorize how you use things: to drink, to eat, to open with a can opener or tear open yourself or crack open, to wash your dishes or wash your clothes or wash your face or wash your toilet or wash your floor, to peel, to refrigerate or freeze, to eat the way it is, to cook.

- Talk about where things come from: eggs, produce from on top of the ground or underneath the ground or from a tree, hamburger, ham, fish, bread, spaghetti.

- Count how many different colors of napkins or paper plates there are on the shelf. See if there are more white napkins or colored napkins or patterned napkins.

- See how many brands there are of cereal, of coffee, of butter.

- Count packages that have the color pink or red or green.

- Look for the smallest jar you can find, then the biggest can.

- Note the various flavors of ice cream and decide what might be in them.

- Speculate which people in the store are working there.

- Search for shoppers wearing jackets, jeans, crocs, bumper-sticker t-shirts.

- Compare if there are more men or women or children in the store. More children walking or riding in carts.

- Look for the fullest cart. Can you spot anyone carrying just a hand basket?

- Count the number of aisles.

This should last you for at least a month. Next month you'll be making your own list.

It is not your job description to entertain your child 100% of the time. It's not even recommended since your child does need to make a life of his own.

But when it's practical, make your time with him productive and fun. It can open the doors of his mind, as well as your own.

Television and computers probably can absorb your child for hours. There are many wonderful things children can learn from them, and many long hours children can be entertained by them, thus many free moments you can have to yourself (or to clean the kitchen). Reasonable use of television and computers does no harm as long as the content is appropriate. But they, like any other life activity, can never take the place of you. You are the center of the world for your child. Enjoy while you can, knowing it will not always be so.

Wonderful commercial toys lure children and they can be a great addition to your child's life. Never think buying stuff for your child is enough...never, never, never. And this is good. Have you ever bought a big toy for your young child's birthday...and watched him open the package, look at the toy, put down the toy, and play with the box? Children sense the importance of real life. Computers and television and movies and toys, even playgroups and swimming pools and soccer games, are hollow if they are a substitute for your time, for your attention, for your love, for *you*.

As the adult in charge, you set the pace for living. Life offers many wonderful things for each of you to do. But overchoice can lead to overscheduling can lead to overwhelmed. If things get too frantic, you slow them. It isn't always easy to limit activities, especially once commitments are made (soccer teams, room mother, piano lessons). Limiting, however, is easier than having your household implode. At least project for the very near future a schedule that allows time for family, time for home living and laughing and loving. Soccer may last through third grade, perhaps even through high school, but it's not a substitute for a family. A family should last forever, and you are the designated person to make that happen. Prioritize commitments to the benefit of both your child and his family.

You may feel that you just don't have time for one more assignment…one more game to play with your child, one more activity to undertake, one more idea from this book. Surprisingly, the activities suggested here will save you time…yes, save you time! Being proactive can produce good behavior and eliminate bad behavior. Instead of nagging, you can have fun. For example, instead of prodding prodding prodding your child to "stop fooling around and get dressed," think of a fun way to make it happen. Hide your eyes and see if you can guess whether he put on his shirt or his pants, his left shoe or his right shoe; he'll be eager to fool you…and he'll get dressed. Crisis averted, job done, and you won't have made three trips to his bedroom to hassle.

Your child will be won over, enjoying the great benefit of his family. You will be a stronger influence than any TV/movie star or singer, than any toy or game, than any peer, than any outside lure or role model.

A worthy goal is sustaining a relationship with your child. Necessarily it starts with you. Give your child an accurate view of the world. Be credible as you guide him to realize his place in that world. Build up as many credits as you can now for being savvy, because in a few years your opinions may be discounted. Your credibility will probably resurface after his teenage years.

Young children have fears. You interpret for your child what is or is not safe. He should believe there is nothing to fear when you tell him there is nothing to fear. He thinks there is someone scary in his room at night? You could give him a flashlight to reassure or at least distract him. You could give him a tape recording (or whatever latest electronic miracle device you have and he can use) with your voice: reading his favorite story, singing his favorite songs, or just talking to him. You could even give him a squirt bottle with water, colored or scent added, to spray away anything scary he might envision in his room. But the underlying reassurance should be your realistic assurance that it is safe, and if there were danger *you would tell him*—just as you tell him it's not safe to run out into traffic, just as you tell him not to touch the hot stove, just as you tell him to wear a bicycle helmet. You establish over a period of time the level of trust between yourself and your child.

More than hearing your words of reassurance,

your child will get courage from your courage. (Remember that true courage is not braggadocio, but a little boasting may be a necessary first and temporary step for a fearful child.) Every day we can be confronted with difficult situations—little ones and even great big ones. Show your child you have the confidence that you, and he, will get through. We all can be The Little Engine that Could.

Good grief, don't quiver at thunder and lightning. Don't tremble when your child has a hard day at school. Don't fret when he doesn't get invited to a friend's party. Don't have a breakdown when his old bike isn't as nice as the neighbor's. Don't shrink if you have to discipline him. This is life, and you can do this—and so can he.

When things get really tough, character does indeed count. Our greatest heroes stood tall to face ill winds. In biographies of many of our heroes, they credit a mother or a grandmother or a father or a mentor for giving them the grit to succeed. One of our distinguished United States Supreme Court Justices has said, "I am fortunate to have known misfortune." Display the faith and confidence that you will triumph. It may take all the courage you can gather, but you can do this. In fact you must do it not only for yourself, but for your child.

Perception can change your child's world, even when the world stays the same. And it is you who lays the groundwork for a winning perception. This approach is not to deny there can be serious problems and concerns about your child.

If the concern is one of chronic or acute special needs, consult professionals. And remember, we all have special needs.

In any of these life circumstances, your creativity can improve the situation and give your child an advantage.

Summary

Of all the world's advantages a child might have, the greatest is a wise and loving adult—*you.*

Your perception of the world is passed to your child.

How your child functions can be perceived in various ways. Unless there is a serious problem, view him in the most respectful and admiring way. A functioning scale can help you formulate productive perceptions.

The purpose of this book is to jumpstart your creativity. There isn't always a ready answer to every child rearing question. Instead of Q and A, it's more like trial and error. Your lucid thinking can reduce instances of error, and your creativity can make it fun.

The goals you have for your child should be clear in your own mind. Conflicting values are confusing.

Overscheduling can be a family burden. Make time for family activities.

Using proactive measures actually saves you time and eliminates stress.

Trust between you and your child is a cornerstone of happy relations.

Get grit.

You can be your child's *Greatest Advantage*.

SECTION VII.

CONCLUSION

A VERY HAPPY ENDING

PREVIEW

If you have given your child an advantage, there will be "A Very Happy Ending." It is right and necessary that we conclude with a discussion that life is precious and that we are indeed fortunate.

These musings help separate the meaningful from the mundane.

Most of all, this section, sometimes with tongue in cheek and sometimes with a tear in the eye, emphasizes perspective. The age-old question, "What is the meaning of life?" finds answers here.

IN ALL THIS, WHERE DID I LOSE MYSELF

Before the birth of your first child, you know you're going to love him. You can have no idea how deeply you will love him. With his first breath, your life is changed forever.

Think back. You lost part of yourself the first time you held that child. You lost your heart to that child. It's odd about a heart; you gladly give it away, but it still swells with pride inside you.

Since that first time with your baby, you may also have lost sleep, privacy, time, money, social engagements, perhaps even any sense of decorum. You've surely lost modesty. No doubt, you've lost all sense of objectivity.

As time goes by, you lose other things.

In one of our centers, at the end of the day, a father was signing out his two-year-old. As Dad was attending to that state-required task, his son kept running away. A teacher, observing the would-be escapee, asked the exhausted father, "Don't you wonder where he gets all his energy?" Father answered in gasps, "I know where he got it…he drained it from me."

Eventually you may lose your organized house, your television rights, your computer, and any hope of quiet time before midnight, perhaps even your self-confidence and more money. Is it worth the price? You know it is!

With every child, your first to your last, you lose things and you gain things.

You meet new people: the pediatrician, the pharmacist, the ladies of the la leche group, the parents in the support group, the families in play group, the financial planner, the life insurance sales person. In time the mini-gym coach, the piano teacher, the language teacher, the dance teacher, the soccer coach, the preschool teacher, Chuck E Cheese, the realtor when you need a larger house, the loan officer at the bank. Do you see how your horizons are expanding?

You have new interests and hobbies: collecting Pampers coupons, assessing the quality of various cotton swabs, monitoring the effects of different laundry detergents, comparing pacifiers (and searching for them when they are lost—a parent version of Hide and Seek).

You broaden your reading habits: following mixing instructions for baby formula, studying the ingredient lists on baby food products, searching for Fifth Disease symptoms on the computer, comparing and contrasting diverse recommendations from multiple child expert authors, examining the fine print regarding safety and use of baby equipment (cribs, bouncers, bottle warmers), scanning instruction manuals to assemble strollers and swings, studying specific requirements for admission to the best preschools. Note the ongoing expansion of your education.

Fast forward. Now you've lost your car (at least on Friday nights), any hope of relaxation before he gets home, maybe some of your best clothes and jewelry, any electronic gadget you purchased through Best Buy or Cellular One, your credibility, serenity, certainly more of your money. But you've gained an orthodontist, a school counselor, and at least ten pounds.

So you see, you haven't really lost yourself. You've just lost your old self. You've taken a different road—and what an exciting ride it will be.

WILL MY CHILD GROW UP AND TELL A PSYCHIATRIST ABOUT ME

What could he tell?

...that you adored him.

...that you rocked him and clothed him and fed him.

...that you worried about him and for him.

...that you cheered him up and cheered him on.

...that you taught him and fought him.

...that he wasn't always right and you weren't always right, but neither of you was always wrong.

...that you played games and read books and laughed and hugged.

...that you did the best you could.

...and that you still adore him.

Who wouldn't like to live this story?

Oh sure, there were the times you had to tell him no. And the times you were too busy to pay full attention to him. Oh, well. You needed him to know that he couldn't be the center of the entire world, and sometimes not even the center of his own family.

Children meet their needs by manipulating their caregivers. This is a necessary survival tool, not to be carried on and on indefinitely. Eventually your child will grow up.

He will have limited sad tales to tell if you have taught him a sense of responsibility. At some point in every person's life, he must accept responsibility for his own actions. Even if his upbringing wasn't picture perfect. By the time a person can make an appointment with a psychiatrist, keep the appointment, and pay for it himself, it's time for him to accept responsibility for himself.

Things may be hard. You've taught him grit. If life gives you lemons, make lemonade…and other platitudes. Abraham Lincoln observed that a man is just about as happy as he makes up his mind to be. We recognize the rare instance that calls for more drastic measures, and when that occurs it is proper and advisable to seek professional help. (Such condition is outside the scope of this book. Even desperate situations have their day and can be gotten past, as they usually are.) Life generally can be brought under control when a person "makes up his mind."

Another wise man speculated on attitude:

- The optimist thinks this is the best of all possible worlds.

- The pessimist knows this is the best of all possible worlds.

Deep thinking about the human condition. Where do you stand?

If you've taught your child perspective, it eases

most cases of anguish. You don't have as many things as your friends? Oh, mercy, don't you realize there are children who have no food but do have AIDS. Your girlfriend dumped you? Oh, for goodness sake, there are millions of girls left in this world. You are bored? Clean your room and get a job. You feel insecure? Then do something to help someone else. And don't drink or smoke anything funny; it won't make things better—at least not for long. It could make things a whole lot worse, and it probably will.

If your child is telling his tale of woe, he must acknowledge that during all those heartbreaking times you were there to hold him and to sympathize. Not to wallow, mind you, since your house is a no-wallowing zone.

Does he know that his every disappointment hurt you too? Does he realize that you would have had him be the victor of all? Does he even suspect that it needn't matter? Does he know what you know?

You know that no person has it all. Your child can strive for excellence in his own life, without favorable or unfavorable comparisons to others. A steep pyramid holds a few people at the top, having the most money and the most toys and the most celebrity. The cutest girls and the champion jocks and the most popular students and the CEOs. That alone is no guarantee of a good life. At any place along the pyramid people can find love and happiness and job satisfaction and friends and a fulfilling life. The opportunities are unlimited. Your child can form his own definition of what he is. For that, he should be awed and grateful every day of his life—and so should you.

The character and values you have instilled will always surface in him. Any down times will be temporary.

Life is a mixture of cheers and tears. At least if you your child grows up and tells a psychiatrist about you, it will be on his dime. So he probably won't.

HOW DOES IT ALL END

Happily ever after? Probably not always, not every minute of every day.

But it should end with deep satisfaction, with an awareness that life is precious.

Look at your child now. You know there will be good times and bad times. Will you consider the next years as the distress of a rough bumpy road or the thrill of a roller coaster?

You have opened to the beginning of your own book. You have the tools to write your own story. Where will your path with your child go? At each juncture, you make decisions. They won't all lead to the promised land, oh no. Remember it's not the end of the journey but the journey itself that makes up a life.

Just think of the adventures you will have.

How will it all end? With a legacy you have built, year after year, with your work and your love. You will watch your child grow into a wonderful, productive, kind adult—like yourself, yet different, his own person.

In your book you will write a history of holidays and galas, of milestones and events, of everyday victories and defeats. You'll have a list of friends you've made and places you've gone and people you've entertained.

You'll write of first recitals and first ball games and first swim meets and first proms.

You'll also write of broken bones and broken hearts.

You'll have pictures of your child's first steps and the empty space of his first lost tooth.

There will be photos of baptisms and birthdays and confirmations and bar mitzvahs and graduations.

There will be pictures of friends and relatives and neighbors and pets.

Someday there may be pictures of weddings and the birth of a new generation. And then there will be many, many more pictures.

As you begin the early chapters of your life, you cannot realize how quickly the years will pass. Blink your eyes and you'll be far into your book.

When you write your final chapter, tears of joy may stain the pages as you write:

"I know I gave my child an advantage!"

Summary

Written with a prayer that we use all our blessings to do good.